D0436803

LOVE AND DEATH IN THE SUNSHINE STATE

LOVE
AND
DEATH
IN THE
SUNSHINE
STATE

The Story of a Crime

CUTTER WOOD

ALGONQUIN BOOKS OF CHAPEL HILL   2018

Published by
ALGONQUIN BOOKS OF CHAPEL HILL
Post Office Box 2225
Chapel Hill, North Carolina 27515-2225

a division of
WORKMAN PUBLISHING
225 Varick Street
New York, New York 10014

A NOTE FROM THE AUTHOR: This is the story of a woman's disappearance
in 2008, but it should not be regarded as the complete and unedited truth. Any
number of events have been left out; names have been changed; the fullness of the
moon has been reconstructed; human beings have been collapsed into composite
characters; certain scenes have been shifted and condensed while others, which
occurred with a pace more conducive to the story, were allowed to remain
relatively intact; and I have relied on my own imperfect powers of apprehension
and comprehension, on the narrative norms of our culture, and on the vagaries
of memory. Add to this the essentially amorphous nature of language, and the
truth—that outrageous and delightful hubbub—can seem very far away. And
yet, other than chapters 8 through 15, which include my fictionalized
account of events, this book has been based on that truth.

Library of Congress Cataloging-in-Publication Data
Names: Wood, Cutter, author.
Title: Love and death in the Sunshine State : the story of a crime / Cutter Wood.
Description: First edition. | Chapel Hill, North Carolina :
Algonquin Books of Chapel Hill, 2018.
Identifiers: LCCN 2017045041 (print) | LCCN 2017047569 (ebook) |
ISBN 9781616208264 (ebook) | ISBN 9781616207304 (hardcover : alk. paper)
Subjects: LCSH: Musil-Buehler, Sabine, 1959-2008—Death and burial. | Murder—
Investigation—Florida—Case studies. | Murder victims—Florida—Case studies.
Classification: LCC HV6533.F6 (ebook) | LCC HV6533.F6 W66 2018 (print) |
DDC 364.1/523/097596—dc20
LC record available at https://lccn.loc.gov/2017045041

10 9 8 7 6 5 4 3 2 1
First Edition

This unspeakable crime that lies between them is only
the consequence of their ordinary comings and goings,
of an unkind word here, a disappointment there, but
it lies on them as heavily as any vice, as murder.

—JOHN CHEEVER

There is almost nothing that is not brought to a finished
state by means of fire.

—PLINY THE ELDER

I never judged anybody who didn't deserve to be judged.

—WILLIAM CUMBER

CONTENTS

LOVE AND DEATH IN THE SUNSHINE STATE

1:   Convalescence in the Greater Tampa Bay Area

THE ISLAND IS ABOUT seven miles long. Nowhere is it higher than ten feet above sea level, and at its widest, it is hardly a thousand yards across. It floats like a shinbone in the Gulf of Mexico, so long and flat and narrow that when seen from a distance, the land hardly interrupts the surface of the water.

Still, there are houses on Anna Maria. Several thousand people live there, and many more rent bungalows or rooms so they can spend some portion of their year in such proximity to the sea. The back of the island is laced with dead-end canals, and though you have to drive to Cortez, over on the mainland, to find anyone who actually fishes for a living, the island's many boats and docks keep the idea vivid. When the tide goes out, the cement walls of the canals reveal a crusting of algae and oyster shells, and at dawn someone is always motoring for deeper water. One might as well fish. There isn't much else to do.

The motel remains in my mind exactly as it was that first January: small and dreary and bright. A few pale-yellow buildings squatted in the sun while above them a handful of spindly palms nodded in conference. In a cage by the office door, a green parrot carried on its endless and solitary conversation. Aside from myself, there were only two other people present, a teenaged girl at the reception desk erasing answers from a crossword, and an old German woman folding towels severely in a latticed hut by the pool. The room I was given was sparsely furnished. In one corner, a small black refrigerator rattled off the minutes of the afternoon. A comforter splotched in pastels had been spread across the bed, and lying there, I could almost reach out and flush the toilet.

My college graduation had occurred a few months previously, a celebratory event that had left me in a state of highly animated confusion. In all my years of education, in that succession of desks, in the thousands of cumulative hours stationed before them, and in the countless fancies I'd entertained there, head turned, eyes drawn through the window to the trees beyond, I had somehow failed to foresee that moment when, dressed in a black cap and gown, I would no longer be going to school. During that abortive Floridian vacation, ostensibly a visit with extended family, I spent much of each day adrift in their talk, conversations that passed through various topics but eventually returned to the essential touchstones of real estate and physical ailments and the weather up north. At some moment, someone said we had better hit the beach if we wanted to catch the sunset, and as I walked along the sand trailing those familiar figures, I had the sensation of a return to childhood. The flatness of the sea, the incessant back-and-forth of the waves: these seemed to have been called up from another time, and as we picked our way around the ruins of sandcastles, with the waves measuring out the hours, I felt an acute uneasiness. Sidestepping the dissolving turrets and towers with their seaweed flags, I thought I saw in those shapes the futility of all human efforts, and by substituting *human* for *my*, I was able almost entirely to sidestep as well the uncomfortable topic of my own futile efforts.

There had been no place for me at the family house, so I had taken a room at the motel. I spent the nights on my own, taking long forced marches up and down the streets, and sitting on my bed with a book or the local paper and a Styrofoam container of fried mullet, maligning the future that refused to coalesce warm and graspable before me. The utter inanity of the trip was crystallized by a visit to a distant relative in St. Petersburg on our final day. An old Italian man, he concluded the tour of his home by walking me out to the dock. The bay stretched out before us, and a large blue heron cocked its head at our approach.

"She comes every day," he said. "It's my mother's spirit." He reached out a hand. The bird turned one eye on the empty palm, spread its wings with disdain, and flew off across the water. He shrugged. "Usually I bring capicola."

Toward the end of January, I left with no intention of ever returning to the island or the state, and this would have been the case, I think, if some months later I had not received in the mail a clipping from the Anna Maria newspaper. A grainy color photograph showed a few palms outlined against a mass of fire. Sent by my mother, it was a story about the burning of the motel where I'd been a guest.

The evening of the fire had been unusually cold, according to the article. There was a strong wind, and the sky was empty of clouds. As the sun began to drop into the Gulf, the water turned bronze, and a woman driving home didn't understand at first how the sun could be reflected so brightly in the windows of the motel. Only when she drew near did she realize it was flames.

As happens sometimes at the lower latitudes, it was dark before anyone realized, and when the fire department arrived shortly after seven, one of the motel's buildings was wholly engulfed. The roof groaned. The palms crackled and swayed. The wind came in steady off the water, carrying smoke across the island, and for blocks around, the air had the sharp smell of melted plastic and polyester. Their gear clanking, a few firefighters walked the perimeter to assess the situation, while the rest began the work of unfurling the heavy hoses and loosening the hydrants' caps. A crowd had already begun to form: couples out for a sunset stroll, retirees on their way home from an early dinner, children on bicycles and scooters with nothing better to do. Soon a car from the sheriff's office arrived, and a thin deputy began asking the onlookers, for their own safety, to step back, please, and allow the crew to do its work.

The rumor of arson always attends a fire, and this was no exception. The crowd murmured, and when a van pulled up from the local TV station it was clear the reporter hadn't come to tell a story about an accidental blaze. The deputy smoothed the air with his hands. This was a fire, nothing more and nothing less, and there was not yet any reason to believe it was a case of arson. But, he said, you had to admit it was suspicious, considering the circumstances.

The circumstances, in the most immediate sense, were a white 2000 Pontiac convertible. It belonged to one of the owners of the motel, a woman named Sabine Musil-Buehler, and it currently sat in the sheriff's impound lot. It was not a particularly nice car, but it contained a good deal of blood, and this, combined with the fact that the woman had been missing for nearly two weeks, gave a certain amount of credence to the more macabre fantasies of the crowd. As the fire department began sending sprays of water onto the building's roof, an elderly woman still dressed in her pajamas declared that she was frightened and was leaving the island this instant, and for a long while after, she continued to make this declaration to anyone in earshot. It was hard not to stay around and skim the gossip. Who had set the fire, after all, and more importantly, why? For a time, the onlookers pursued these questions, picking up the various theories, turning them this way and that, and putting them back down again. But it was a cold night for Florida, and windy, and getting late, and there are limits to what reasonable people can be expected to ask themselves after dark. A little past eight, the fire chief declared the blaze under control, and the people, in ones and twos, began picking out paths home along the puddled road. A whole town runs to be present at a fire, as Hazlitt notes, but the spectator hardly exults to see it extinguished.

2:   In Search of Another

BEFORE I CAN BEGIN to explain the fire at the motel, I need to set out a few notes on the months preceding it, the summer and fall of 2008, when, with high anticipation, I left my job waiting tables and enrolled in the graduate program at the University of Iowa as a student of creative nonfiction. I arrived in Iowa City early one morning in August 2008 feeling an ecstasy that now seems to me to presuppose endeavors of great idiocy. A quick overview of my belongings illustrates the lack of forethought with which I approached my new life: a pair of jeans, a pair of sneakers, a number of collared shirts of the loose-fitting mainsailish variety still popular in the hinterlands of Pennsylvania, a toothbrush, an exact replica of Charles Dickens's traveling desk and a wholesale box of Alka-Seltzer (presents both from my woodworker father), a dull kitchen knife, two dozen identical black notebooks, all blank, and an elaborate oak four-poster bed, acquired at a rummage sale, which I quickly discovered would not fit up the stairs to my apartment. And in an act that far too accurately encapsulates the delusional nature of both my romantic and literary expectations, I spent my first hour in Iowa sawing my bed into pieces.

That day, having piled the pieces of my bed in the middle of my apartment and swept the sawdust off the front stoop with my foot, I set off to explore the city, heading first, as seemed natural, for the river. I followed the lacy shadows of a line of sycamores, taking in the academic buildings, the meadowy greens, the solitary beaver chugging upstream. I eyed the long-legged silhouettes of the women's crew team, who even at that early hour were already hauling in their boats and hosing the thick sludge of manurish grime off the gunwales. Then, turning my steps back toward the city, I passed quickly through the few blocks of shops and bars downtown and walked, as I have always loved to do, down the alleys of the residential neighborhoods. In the unkempt backyards of late summer, a rose clung to the side of a garage, a melon ripened in the sun, and a boy and his sister played alone with an axe, and even in those first hours, I thought I saw in the place, in the shape of its houses and the largesse of its sky, a sense of proportion entirely pleasing to the eye. I climbed the only hill, a mound of dirt at the top of which sat the charming prairie bungalows of the professors, and standing on those red brick streets, I momentarily attained something that was not quite a vista, more a sense of pleasant and gentle removal from the life I was about to begin living. I stood looking down toward the city and imagined myself, acclaimed yet charmingly, almost heroically, humble.

The apartment I'd rented was on the second floor of a vinyl-sided Victorian at the corner of Fairchild and Dubuque Streets, and I had rented it for the sole reason that it possessed a turret, which seemed to me so emblematic of the artistic mantle I was to take up that months prior to moving I'd begun using the house as my return address. In my turret, I assumed my position at the Dickens desk, spread open a fresh notebook, wrote the day's date at the top of the page, and, with windows looking in every direction, meditated heftily on the great work that no doubt would begin to emanate from me at any moment. In this position, I was able to witness the very ebb and flow of university life. My turret was a sort of poop deck on the sea of the student unconscious, and already on that first day, as my own thoughts quickly proved barren and dull, I allowed myself to be drawn out into the lives of those walking below: a woman struggling to roll a purple suitcase over the uneven sidewalk; a man on roller skates; my landlord, a nearsighted lawyer, talking to his mother on a cell phone. Late that evening, in a prelude to what was to become a nightly ritual, a young couple walked home on opposite sides of the street, shouting "Cunt!" (him) and "Pussy!" (her) at one another until, a block beyond my apartment, they reunited in Bergman-Bogart fashion beneath a flickering streetlamp for a cephalopodic embrace, the slopping sound of which, at that distance, by holding my breath, I could just hear.

Looking back on my notebooks from that time, I am filled with a throat-clearing flush of chagrin. When I see again the exuberant young man in heavy orthopedic-looking tennis sneakers, installing himself with his pen and practiced scowl in the front window of a coffee shop, devoted to the great conversation of literature

with such impatient zeal that he could hardly string two para-
graphs together, it is as if, looking at some old photographs, I've
discovered I had a lazy eye in elementary school. And indeed,
in all the many pages I filled then, there was barely a sustained
thought in evidence:

Along with milk, I am thinking of writing about the war in Iraq.

Or, after finding an earring in a pool of blood on the sidewalk:

Why is it that blood always seems like it should be cleaned up?

Or, the closest I ever came to prescience, this koan-like fragment:

The great discrepancy between what comes to me and what I
write down is

I had no inkling at the time, but I was that classical caricature,
a devotee less of writing than of imagining, of holding thoughts
in an ideal illiterate state, where they seem to shudder with the
promise that, once one actually takes up the pen, immediately
vanishes. Those first weeks, there was a great deal of writing in
my notebooks about the behavior of the sparrows that squabbled
over crumbs outside the cafés, and patiently transcribed carnal
dreams in which I played a starring role, and lengthy descriptions
of my meals (the corn-on-the-cob odes, while somewhat wordy,
are not wholly without merit), but there was little that surpassed
the length of a paragraph.

At times, circumstances arrange themselves in perfect concord
with our desires, even if those desires remain obscure to us, and
within a few weeks of my arrival, as I began to feel the need to escape from Iowa and the life I'd embarked upon there, I received

a voicemail message, which proceeded in the emotionally oblique manner so natural to my family:

> Hi, Cutter.
>
> It's your dad. Hope you're writing up a storm out there. I just wanted to call and let you know your grandfather's not doing well. He stopped eating, and it looks like he won't hold out much longer.
>
> Otherwise, everything here is proceeding pretty much apace. We're working on getting your grandfather's house back in shape, and there hasn't been any trouble since I started the resettlement program. At first, I was just taking them down to the river, but then I started thinking they could probably find their way back, so now I'm driving the squirrels across the river and dropping them at the top of the mountain. I took two gray ones Sunday and a red one Monday—the red ones, as you know, are particularly wily. It's only two miles, but I'm hoping the river's enough to keep them from coming back. I don't expect they'll try to swim it. Of course, I wouldn't put it past them to use the bridge; although it's fairly exposed, that's just the sort of thing they'd do.
>
> It does always make me nervous, driving over with them in the trap in the back seat. I haven't heard them plotting revenge yet, but any moment I figure I'll look in the rearview and see a squirrel head suddenly pop up—you've seen that look they get in their eyes—and that'll be the end.
>
> *A great sigh.*
>
> That's really the disadvantage of a hatchback—no trunk to keep squirrels in.

I had a dream last night that woke me up, the kind of dream you'd have when your dad is dying. Then I couldn't get back to sleep, and there are these couple of lines of a poem—all my long drives I get these words sorting themselves out in my head—and I just laid there, not sleeping and rolling these lines around, and then I started thinking about cleaning out the attic. I figured with squirrels living there for the past forty years, there'd be walnut shells about two feet deep, but now that I'm up here there aren't even two thousand, I bet. Maybe twenty-five hundred.

Birdsong interrupts.

All right, bud, sorry to bend your ear so long. We're going to bring your grandfather back from the hospital this week so he can die at home. I hope you'll come for the service. The walnut trees are losing their leaves. Why don't you give a call tonight at dinner so you can talk to your mom.

HAVING DRIVEN NEARLY fourteen hours across the plains in a rented car, I arrived in Muncy, Pennsylvania, a few days before the funeral to find the clouds being hauled in piles across a wide turquoise sky, and the wind blowing yellow beech leaves down the highway ahead of me. At the end of Main Street, where the curbs disappeared and the sidewalk abruptly ended, my grandfather's house sat on its hump of clay above the river, shaded by walnut and ash trees. The brick walls and white trim, scaled with moss, gave it the look of a place that had moldered through a century or two and intended to go on moldering for a few centuries more. The house was empty when I arrived, doors open so that the wind swept down the narrow front hall, through the rooms, and out into the backyard, and in some corner a radio had been left on and was playing a tinny big-band tune. I followed a low *chuck-chuck* sound into the grove of lilacs and raspberry brambles behind the house and found my mother standing on the back porch.

"Your father's in the crawl space," she said, nodding at a small dark doorway halfway up the side of the house. It was a room hardly tall enough for a child to stand up straight in. It contained, as my father later termed it, "the walnut motherlode," and while we couldn't see him from where we stood, every few seconds a shovelful of walnut hulls flew from the doorway and landed in the yard.

My mother held a small coffee cup, part of my grandmother's old green-and-white Corelle set. She'd filled it three-quarters full with gin. "Can you believe this?" she said, nodding up toward my dad. "I can't believe it. He's shoveling walnuts when he should be making funeral arrangements. This looks just like a big pile of shit." She sipped meditatively, then called up at the house, "Jim! This looks like a pile of shit down here, you know." She sighed and drank again. "I couldn't find the martini glasses. It's nice to see you, honey."

In the twenty-four hours that preceded the funeral, my father absorbed himself in a flurry of senseless activity. He ripped out all the closets in the house and began to put up new drywall, bought and returned a series of dressers, mowed the lawn, harvested beans by flashlight, purchased a chain saw, and ironed a single tie over and over again. And he left behind him in every room he visited something that he'd inexplicably been carrying: one of his many tape measures, a pistol from the Civil War, a box of lead soldiers, the chain saw's crumpled instruction manual, handfuls of rusted square-head nails, sketches for a calendar that, by a series of rotations, could be used forever, his good shoes.

The morning of the funeral, the sky opened up suddenly, and the assembled family sat trapped in the summer kitchen watching the rain pour down. I had just received my first pair of eyeglasses, and every object seemed to stand out with an almost crystalline clarity. Limbs of walnut and lilac, their bark mottled with lichen, had been stacked beside the fireplace and gave off a pungent, mossy perfume as the flames warmed them. Coffee and bourbon circulated, along with plates of warm peach custard pie, beside which the vanilla ice cream had gone glossy and begun to pool. The rain fell very precisely into the grass and disappeared, and every so often, the wind blew the trees, and the tin roof resounded with a rifle-crack report. "Walnuts," my father said under his breath.

I ducked back into the house to sit alone in my grandfather's office. Behind his desk was a swivel chair of orange burnished leather, which squealed on its casters when I dragged it into the middle of the room. That morning, I sat in the chair and, as I'd often done as a boy, spun myself slowly in circles. It seemed to me that the burial would be an almost-perfunctory act. Those my grandfather had loved, to whatever degree he was able, had mostly preceded him. The last decade of his life, he'd already tenanted a world populated mostly by ghosts, and in death he only made official what had previously been, as he would have said, ipso facto. His few remaining friends would sit in the chairs nearest the grave, waiting their turn. Neither then, as I spun listlessly in circles, listening to the rain, nor for a long while after did it occur to me that much of the grieving after a death is done not so much for the loss of the loved one but for the simple passage of time, which so gently obliterates everything before it.

At the funeral, five nearly identical great-grandsons were tucked like dolls into their suits and seated one after another in the pew with lemon candies in their mouths and their feet dangling above the tile floor. Old men were helped to their feet, spoke, and sat down. "I was stationed in North Africa when I sent Tom Wood a letter by V-mail. That's *V-mail*, not *email*. It was February 19, 1943, a Friday . . ." The organist sat facing the chancel, shoulders hunched beneath a wide lace collar.

The entire day bent itself toward that hole in the ground, and when the grave finally lay open before us, the uneasy relationship of the living to the dead was summed up not by the pastor, who cleared his throat and lowered his eyes, saying, "Yea, though I walk through the valley of the shadow of death," but by one of the grave-digging crew, a man with a camouflage cap and a ruffle of brown hair hanging halfway down his back. His sneakers were dirty with the muck of the grave, and he'd misbuttoned his shirt so that one side of his collar sat higher than the other. Beneath it, a hunter-orange fabric showed out. As the pallbearers approached with the casket, he stood at the head of the hole, holding his hands out parallel before him saying, "Square her up, y'all . . . Square her up . . ."

THE EFFECT OF the death of a person does not necessarily correlate with how well you knew them or whether you bore them any affection. No one can say whether the funeral of an aunt will plunge you into deepest depression or profoundest meditation, or will only take up four hours of the afternoon. You may sleep as softly as a child that night, wake chipper, and breakfast on potato salad and hot egg sandwiches on a patio covered in wisteria, and two hours later be brought to your knees with despair at the sight of a little clubfooted pigeon in the gas station parking lot. Or the grief, if grief even is the right word, will manifest itself only years or decades later, as an inability to eat the licorice your aunt always ate, the smell of which seemed to exude from her very skin.

In my case, I slipped away from the wake, declining the plate of fried chicken and the slice of watermelon, and drove around in the rain until I'd found a hotel bar where I felt I could be certain of seeing no one I'd ever known. I sat with a book and tried to make some sense of the tumult of the past weeks. In the lobby, a stream of old Indian women in gaily colored saris were passing back and forth between the restroom and a wedding in the banquet hall across the way, and through the open doors, I could just make out the bride and groom as they were led in a circle by an officiant with a Rasputinish glare. At each successful circumnavigation of the marriage bower, he paused, looked gravely at the crowd, and said, "Please make them a hand." A hesitant applause followed. The saturated shades of the women's garments, cerulean and crimson and chartreuse; the eyes of the officiant glowering beneath his brow; and the murmurs of the wedding, sounding to my ear like a kind of musical drowning: it was against this background that I attempted to come to terms with the death of a man I'd both respected and despised, the Honorable Thomas Wood, judge in the Lycoming County Court of Common Pleas.

Well before I was born, my grandfather had been elected to the court, a position that, to preserve the objectivity of the office, came with a ten-year term. He lived with my grandmother in the dilapidated farmhouse in Muncy, and Monday to Friday he drove the fifteen miles to Williamsport to sit for cases ranging from divorce to delinquency to the fluoridation of the water supply. He was highly regarded, I'd been told at the funeral, lenient in his sentences and ahead of his time in his notions of justice, and after we'd lowered the casket into the grave, a stooped old man had pulled me aside to say there was never anyone as honest and compassionate as Judge Wood.

I spent a great deal of my childhood with only my grandparents as company, and one would have thought that I'd have sensed that honesty and compassion. A photograph I have above my desk shows my grandfather kneeling beside me in the grass in front of a broken lawn mower. I am perhaps three or four as his hand guides mine. But my memory had retained little from those earliest years, and as I sat in the hotel bar watching the wedding couple circle the bower yet another time, I could recall only the man whose sharp tongue had often been employed against those closest to him.

After my grandmother's death, he had decided that the two of us would travel together to England, and I remembered those miserable weeks in the British Isles in livid detail. I a giddy twelve, he eighty-two and sliding into dementia, we composed in my memory an almost comic pair, the old man obstinate and furious and wandering aimlessly across cobble and heath, through fog and rain, and behind him the gangly boy, helpless and near tears, pleading with him to stop, turn around, this was not the way to the hotel. He had given me my first journal in anticipation of that trip, a hardcover notebook clothbound in black linen with clean cream paper, and it was on those pages that I'd recorded my earliest written pledge to the task of honesty:

> I fear I have been avoiding writing my feelings so as not to hurt the feelings of others, and I will continue to do so, <u>I must</u>, but I will try to chart as many of my feelings as possible. I would rather remember how things felt than what time we got up in the morning.

These feelings, about which I felt so strongly, were by and large feelings of utter loathing for my traveling companion. On that trip, removed by only a few months from my grandmother's death and forced for weeks on end into my grandfather's capricious company, I had begun to understand all too well how, subjected for decades to his ire, she might have slipped so meekly from this life. The journal ended as we dined with his acquaintances. In a much-draped room, over a meal of haggis, my grandfather quizzed me on my knowledge of literature, and having satisfied himself with my ignorance, suggested to the assembled company that if I really wanted to write, I should be given five hundred dollars and put out on the street. *I hated him,* I wrote (I could not muster the courage to use the present tense). *I just hated him.*

So lost was I in my recollection of his indictment and of that fragile pubescent era, which seemed in retrospect like some awful foreshadowing of my future failures, that the appearance of a woman in the doorway of the banquet hall hardly stirred my attention. Only as she crossed the lobby did she begin to edge into my consciousness. She wore a tube dress, coral pink, and yellow heels on which she tottered with a studied care, and as my eyes regained their focus, it was as if the memory of those middle-school years

had produced a figure of its own accord. In one of those eerie for-
tuities of small-town life, I recognized this woman at once—taller
but with the same sharp chin, the darkly circled eyes, the long,
faintly freckled Parisian nose—as my now-grown seventh-grade
crush.

"Erin," I said.

"Oh," she said. "Cutter. I have to pee so bad."

As she swept past, bracing herself on the bar for support, it was
as if a ghost had been resurrected, and I felt a sense, as I hadn't in
some time, of life's purpose. I busied myself looking at my book,
and she appeared again a few minutes later and took the stool beside me.

"Good wedding?" I said.

"Oh, a friend of a friend." She leaned over and took the book
from my lap. "*Beowulf*? That's very old-fashioned of you."

"It's gory," I said. "Bones cracking, heads getting cut off, the
limitless woe of Hrothgar. Really great."

"This is going to sound stupid," she said, wrinkling her nose.
"But I think I thought it had wolves in it."

In Iowa City, in the company of aspiring writers, arguments
could burst into being and friendships could be broken by merely
mentioning the work of Baudelaire in a roomful of people who
had never read a single line of his poetry. The week before, I had
spent two excruciating hours pretending to have read a number of
Montaigne's essays, excusing myself from time to time to use the
bathroom, where in the cramped stall I would pull out my phone
and absorb everything I could on the ponderous Frenchman.

It may have been her disarming statement, it may have been the
thoughts of my grandparents or the harpsichord music drifting

from the lobby, or it may only have been the whiskey, but looking at Erin, as she stood at my shoulder, mouthing the words on
the open page of my book (*A few miles from here a frost-stiffened
wood waits and keeps watch above a mere . . .*), I seemed to see her
as through a caul, and with hardly any sense of what I was doing,
I said to her, "You know, I had a terrible crush on you in seventh
grade."

"Yeah." She looked up from the book. "I guess I had a crush
on you, too."

I knew then how the soldier feels when the grenade lands
squarely in his lap. She settled onto the stool beside me, and we
covered the intervening years quickly. And as effortlessly as I'd
lost it during my first weeks in Iowa, I resurrected that ideal
image of myself: the ascetic, sensitive, diligent writer; victim of
great emotions; haver of excellent thoughts. I offered some dar-
ing little vignettes of the writing life. I put two extra windows
on my turret. She, in turn, offered a charming description of the
city of Pittsburgh, where she currently lived in an apartment of
five people—one, a drunk who regularly collapsed in a pool of his
own urine on the kitchen floor. She made ends meet with a variety of jobs: running the register at a café, supervising a gymnastics camp, dog-sitting. Half her week, she taught at the Carnegie
Museum of Art, a job that allowed her free rein of the museum's
collection, and as she sat on the stool next to me now, our knees
nearly touching, she described in great detail her most recent area
of interest: Abbey's hallucinatory *Penance of Eleanor* and its division of the world into black, white, and red. I had eaten lunch with
this woman every day when we were twelve, and as she spoke,
I found each gesture of her hand, each raising of her eyebrows

unerringly familiar, and though I can't remember now how the conversation led us out of the bar, Erin holding her heels in one hand, me carrying our two whiskeys, I recall well the events that followed. We had decided to reenact a challenge from our childhood, a simple footrace. We walked to the end of an empty hall, and setting my drink down on the floor, I looked up to see her already sprinting away.

As I drew even with her, she threw a shoulder into me, sending me careening against the wall, but it was a glancing blow and I slipped past easily. How different was this sprint from our youthful ones. Flushed with whiskey and exertion, I seemed to glide down the hall, my feet only grazing the carpet. I was maybe ten strides ahead of her when I turned to look back. She streaked toward me, still pumping her arms. Her dark hair streamed behind her, her mouth was set and her fists were clenched, and as I watched, one of her feet just nicked the heel of the other. In an instant, her legs had tangled beneath her, she looked up at me with a kind of perplexity, and her body launched into the air.

During this airborne moment, as she floated down the hallway, her body perfectly parallel to the ground, her high heels preceding her, past a framed still life of daisies and grapes, past a teenaged bellhop with his first hint of mustache, I saw her seventh-grade self, the young girl still in the heyday of a gymnastics career. She had shown an extraordinary talent for the sport, particularly on the bars, where for a time she'd held some notable rank. And more to the point, she had been quite accomplished at tumbling. As she flew down the hall, I imagined her twisting in the air, bouncing, somersaulting, and landing again on her feet, but her impact with the industrial hotel carpet, sudden and calamitous, brought with it only the *oof* of unexpectedly expelled breath. She slid, rolled to a stop at my feet, and looked up at me. I looked back at her, the bell-hop grinned at both of us sleepily, and only then did she realize that the friction of the rug had peeled her dress down to her waist as neatly as a banana.

What hope was there for me then? There lay before me a fully formed woman, flushed, panting, knees bloodied, hair tousled as if by cherubs. I wanted to lie down at her side like a dog and whimper over her wounds, and I hardly knew how I came to be kneeling beside her, at a bench in one of the lobby's little alcoves, between two large potted ferns, holding her shoes in one hand, looking into two eyes that brimmed with tears, not of pain but of surprise. I was smitten, and I felt very valiant as with little puffs of Bactine (offered by the bellhop), I moistened her skinned knees.

Love, of course, always has its impediments. In this case, seven hundred miles. When finally she had to return to the wedding, I placed the bottle of Bactine in her hands, and I said goodbye. I stepped out into the warm, foggy evening and walked the streets for some time, and only late that night, as I lay in the hard bed at my grandfather's house, did I discover that some rough indelible impression had been made on my thoughts, an embossment of her face as she hurtled down the hallway, to which I returned again and again even as I was pulled off into sleep.

A few days later, I returned to Iowa with my inheritance—an ailing Ford Taurus wagon, previously my grandmother's—and a Pittsburgh address in my notebook, and for two months, I sat immobilized and heartbroken as winter bore down.

That December, the wind howled in my turret, the river froze over in the span of a few hours, and one night a storm blanketed the city in ice. Trees, houses, telephone wires, mailboxes, the ranks of abandoned student bicycles: all were covered in a thick gloss of ice, and for days after the storm it was as if we lived our lives in the cold heart of a chandelier. I received occasional letters from Erin and wrote to her in return, the resurrection of a note-passing habit we'd carried on a decade previously. She was delighted to have reconnected after all these years, was grateful for the "intellectual [she could not have used this word unintentionally] stimulation." Confoundingly, so was I. To the face of this woman, once familiar and seen again only for a night, I could return at my convenience, no matter the time of day, and I could imagine whatever I wanted there.

When my mother sent the newspaper clipping, the motel in flames, the palm trees, the disappearance, I made no connection between those events and my own circumstances. But as I read first one article on the case, then another, I felt an uncanny rousing of my interest. In particular, I fixed upon a single detail. The missing woman had kept her pet parrot in the building that had burned, but the fire marshal had not found its bones. It seemed that if someone had murdered Sabine Musil-Buehler and set fire to her motel, he had saved her parrot first. There was something so entirely human in this mixing of good and evil intentions, so familiar, that as I sat in my turret, I had the sudden sense, almost like a shock of static electricity, that I needed to know more. The longer I thought about it, looking out my window at the snow piled in the street, the more certain I became that I had to go to Florida. I had to find out what had happened.

If someone had pointed out to me then that I was using this excursion to distract myself from my own longing for Erin, I would have scoffed. I hummed as I drove, and never once did it cross my mind that having been frustrated in my pursuit of one woman, I had set off in search of another.

3:   The Idea of a Woman

IT'S HARD TO SAY if anyone ever really intended to go to Florida. The soil is poor, the heat unforgiving. The refinement and the social organization of the Maya or the Inca were an impossibility on that peninsula. When de Soto made landfall near Anna Maria, he found only a smattering of warring tribes who wore inflated fish bladders in their ears and built their homes and charnel houses atop vast piles of discarded oyster shells. De Soto himself had believed Florida to contain something it did not, the city of gold, and when he died there after years of searching, I suspect he had begun to realize the vanity of his dream.

The native people most associated with Florida, the Seminole, aren't from there at all. They came to the state only as a last resort during the nineteenth century, when they were forced off the more fertile and temperate lands of Georgia and Alabama. There is something fitting, though, in the Seminole as a state symbol, since any history of Florida is less a history of people arriving there than one of people fleeing somewhere else, Ohio or Germany, or anywhere it happens to be snowing. Like California, it exists for most people as an idea, something to be talked about while you're counting your tips at the end of the night or punching your time card after a graveyard shift. As in de Soto's time, when Florida stretched north unmapped and borderless, the shape of the Sunshine State is defined less by the 31st parallel than by the imagination. Only long after you've arrived, as de Soto discovered, does it become anything like a reality.

To get to Florida from Pennsylvania—where I'd stopped for the New Year to sit briefly in that hotel bar—you follow Interstate 95 down along the Atlantic. At Jacksonville, you cut southwest across the scrub-choked interior of the peninsula, and around Ocala, you turn abruptly south and run parallel to the Gulf Coast for a little over a hundred miles. The Sunshine Skyway Bridge, after its heroic leap across Tampa Bay, eventually deposits you in Bradenton, and by taking the first right turn, you're able to almost entirely avoid that shining, squandered city. You pass the mammoth steel-and-glass Judicial Center, and the old neoclassical courthouse huddled up in its shadow, and then the road opens to four lanes and the buildings shrink away from it, drawing back to allow room for parking lots and billboards. Here are the offices of the orthodontists and cosmetic surgeons, the shake shacks and nail parlors and law firms of one, and the occasional gas station that looks from the mold like it was abandoned decades ago but has been vacant only a few months.

Then the strip stops. Grass replaces the cement sidewalks, and the businesses give way to the long, perfectly smooth walls of the closed communities. Their beige and taupe shells seem to go on forever, interrupted only momentarily by a gate, a guardhouse, a sudden glimpse of ponds, fountains, swans. When at last the walls end, there's the briefest idea of what Florida may have been a long time ago, or of what it will be when it sloughs off its human inhabitants: a solid bank of vegetation borders the road, waxy green and impenetrable. The Florida DOT cuts it back regularly into what looks like a hedge, but behind it there are no homes, no golf courses, no active, unrepentant retirees—only salt marsh and mangrove, ugly lizards and motionless birds, and half-blind crabs the size and color of bruised thumbnails forever sidling in and out of the shadows. Even this, though, is only a flash, and it passes as quickly as a premonition. The sides of the road drop away, and you follow a series of low, simple bridges across the bays and bayous until finally you land on Anna Maria Island, the road Ts, and the only thing left ahead is the Gulf of Mexico.

In January, the island is cold for Florida. The sky clouds over, sometimes for an entire day, and islanders won't put a foot in the surf for another month or two. There are still tourists—there are always tourists—but they are their own breed: the misinformed, the perverse, the congenitally cheapskate. There are some Canadians, a few Swiss. I arrived on a Tuesday.

The motel looked exactly as it had during my last visit—the same German woman in the hut by the pool, the same teen in the office—except off to one side, set a little back from the street, the burned-out building sat, as though hiding, behind two large potted plants. The floor had been swept clean of ash, but long, wavering scorch marks remained on the walls, and police tape flapped between the palms. UNDER CONSTRUCTION said a hand-lettered sign hung on a sawhorse, but there was no evidence to support this notion. In the front office, the girl sat working busily on a sudoku and did not look up when I entered. I asked for the same room I'd rented the previous January, and as I put my clothes in the dresser, removed my shoes, and unwrapped the tiny soap, I felt like in some way I was returning home.

For dinner, I found a restaurant on the beach with a large covered deck, the edge of which disappeared into the sand. All the tables were full, and I took my place on a long bench with the rest of those waiting to eat. To my left was a little boy with a shoe in each hand, pouring sand from one to the other, and to my right sat a man with hair so white and stiff and dramatically windswept it appeared, out of the corner of my eye, as though a seagull sat perched on his head.

It was a popular place to watch the sunset, but by the time I arrived the sky had clouded over. It refused to darken even well after the sun had gone down. Instead, all the objects—the tufts of grass along the beach, the rows of ketchup bottles at the hostess stand, and the plates of half-eaten halibut and shrimp—all these things spread their gloom out around them, and when the whole scene was connected by a single dimness, then it was night. The waitstaff was composed mainly of high school students wearing cutoff shorts and smelling of pimple cream and mall perfume, and older men and women with tobacco-stained fingers. As the first cold breezes blew in off the water, they unrolled large plastic flaps from the ceiling and positioned propane heaters at intervals around the deck, and this combination of the diffuse orange glow of the lamps and the clear plastic walls lent the dining area the distinct feeling of a large and fantastic incubator.

The man to my right finally turned to me. "You from around here?"

Before I could answer, a woman leaned out from behind his shoulder. "We're from Pensacola."

"Pennsylvania," I said. "Originally."

"Never been," said the man. "No reason."

"But I've heard it's lovely," the wife said. "They have the . . . What do you call it? In fall?"

"Foliage."

"Foliage." She sighed over the word. "That's it."

"Here for business?" the husband said.

"I came down to find out about the fire at the motel."

"And the woman that got killed," he said.

"Sabine, yes some people think she was murdered."

"Sabine," said the wife. "Yes, I heard it was her boyfriend."

"True crime," the husband said, inhaling deeply. "You ought to come up to Pensacola. Some unbelievable cases up there. Riots, murders, lynchings . . . Good stuff."

"We should know," the wife said. "Harry's a state prosecutor."

He bowed his head and put out his hand. "Harold and Noreen."

"We're here to get away from his work."

"Lost a case at the state supreme court." He bunched up his shoulders and released them.

"Florida won't execute unless you're the triggerman," Noreen said. "Can you believe it?"

They wanted to say more—a public defender had gotten drunk at a Christmas party and told them things that would make your head spin—but just then, the hostess called their name. Harold shook his head and looked into his drink, and as he pumped my hand a final time, I had my first real glimpse of his face: smooth, almost boyish cheeks and two bright and undiminished eyes.

I made a short dinner of it. The trays of frozen margaritas, the weathered plastic tables, the keenness with which Harold and Noreen had yearned for an execution, and the aging rocker in a corner trying the first chords of a Jimmy Buffett song: all these things had begun to have an oppressive effect on me, and by the time my server arrived, hefting before her a mountainous Caesar salad festooned along its edge with shrimp, I had all but lost my appetite.

After dinner, I walked to a bar down the street. It was a simple stucco building, painted bright blue, with neon beer signs in its small porthole windows. Its dark interior smelled of some solvent, and feeling much more at home, I ordered a whiskey and fell into conversation with the bartender.

Georgia, with the gaunt, cynical forthrightness of a person who ushers her fellow human beings nightly into drink, was happy to lay out any information pertaining to her own life or her perspective on the lives of others. She had come to Florida from Michigan twelve years earlier. For two years, she'd checked the weather on Anna Maria, researching and making sure she was sure, and one day it was just time. She didn't live on the island, of course. Who could afford to live on the island? She lived in one of the developments near Bradenton, a decent enough situation since her ex moved out. And anyway, she got to work here—she gestured down the bar to where two old men drank alone in the dark—on the island. Her hair was teased into a halo around her head, throwing her face into shadow, and when I asked about the missing woman, her eyes narrowed in thought. She leaned against a rack of potato chips and sucked on a cigarette.

"They want to make it out like the boyfriend did it," she said. Gold hoops bounced from her ears as she shook her head. "No way. The husband did it. Follow the money—that's what I say. Barbecue or salt-and-vinegar?" She slid a bag of chips down the bar to one of the old men. "That's two-fifty, honey. Yep, my money's on the husband. It's always the husband. What do you think, Cindy? Who killed that woman that owned the motel?"

Two servers, a man and a woman, had slipped in the back door of the bar. I recognized them from the restaurant.

"Hey," said the woman, glancing at me. "Caesar salad with shrimp."

People who work at restaurants and bars carry on a sort of continual conversation, interrupted sometimes for a minute, sometimes for an hour, by the necessities of their work, and they have developed the skill, through long practice, of sliding into a conversation with fluid ease. Cindy, taking the seat beside me and placing a handful of pens on the bar, didn't balk at Georgia's question or inquire who I was or why we were talking. She only shrugged. "Don't know much about it," she said, and lit a cigarette with one hand while she untied her apron with the other. Forrest, a tall man, folded his apron neatly before him on the counter and took the seat on the other side of her.

"I knew Sabine quite well," he said, his head moving on his neck as if on casters. "We used to make sandcastles together. I'm a little world-famous"—the head swiveled, and he fixed his eyes on me—"in the sandcastle world."

Cindy cut in. "I don't know much about it, but I think the husband killed her and that boyfriend's a patsy. I've always thought so. I mean, how much insurance did they have on that motel?"

"Follow the money," Georgia said, and at this injunction, the three of them drew thoughtfully on their cigarettes. I looked into my glass. On the wall, a white fan nodded back and forth, and at each of its passes, it dispelled the cloud of smoke from around their faces and made Georgia's hair shiver with an anemone-like electricity. "Didn't they used to do nudie camps at the motel, Forrest?" she said.

"Did they?" said Forrest. "It's amazing how you know a person so well, then you just lose track." He leaned behind Cindy and said, "If you'd like, I could show you some sandcastle pictures that would knock your socks off."

"You ever see the husband, Forrest?" said Cindy. "I know you can't tell just from his face if he did it, but did he look like he could've?"

"The husband," Forrest said. "I don't recall."

"The boyfriend story is just too perfect," said Georgia. "And why would he off her with things going good? Over an argument about a cigarette. Ha!"

They all ashed their cigarettes, and Georgia moved the ashtray away and replaced it with a clean one. "I have a fetish about ashtrays," she said, patting a stack of empty ashtrays beside her, and for the first time, she smiled. "Ever since I was a little girl. We never had full ashtrays in my house growing up."

"What about that other guy? Was Corona his name?" said Forrest.

"Yeah, what about him?" said Georgia.

"I don't know anything about him," Cindy said.

"Was it something about money with him?" said Georgia. "Follow the money—that's what I say."

I did not follow the money. I paid for my drinks, thanked them for the conversation, and accepted a business card from Forrest. Then I got in my station wagon and drove over to the mainland. I drove around Bradenton for some time, curious to get a sense of the place, and it was quite late by the time I arrived on Fourteenth Street. At that time of night, the wide empty boulevard felt like a runway. As I parked and stepped out of the car, someone hurried on foot from one side to the other. A sedan streaked by, leaving a greenish line across my retina. There were a few bars, a few motels, some abandoned, some not yet. There was an RV parts-and-repair shop, and a business that rented out inflatable castles, but they'd long since drawn down their metal gates. The pawnshops, too, were closed at that hour. Behind their steel grates were pearlescent guitars, a mounted sailfish, two samurai swords on a stand—the flotsam of misplaced hopes and poor decisions. Even the liquor stores were closed. The bulletproof glass had been wiped clean; its surface smelled of ammonia. Only the gas stations, lit bright like surgeries, were still open at that hour.

It had been on Fourteenth two months earlier, shortly after three o'clock on the morning of November 6, 2008, that a white convertible swung out onto the asphalt. The night was warm but its roof was up, and the radio played loudly. The car traveled a few blocks south—a trip lasting less than a minute—at which point a cruiser from the sheriff's office pulled it over for driving with a broken taillight. The vehicle then turned onto a smaller side street and coasted to a stop on the shoulder of the road.

This part of the city, though only a few miles distant from the coast, was a world away. The houses were small: four walls, a roof, an air conditioner, and a satellite dish. The cruiser came to a stop behind the convertible. The siren and flashers flicked off, and one of the deputies typed in the vehicle's license-plate number. The results came back quickly. The car was registered to an address on Anna Maria Island, to a woman named Sabine Musil-Buehler. But she wasn't the one driving, a fact that became apparent when the door of the convertible opened and a heavyset man wriggled out from behind the steering wheel and ran away.

The deputies radioed for backup, and soon the sheriff's office had set up a perimeter around the area. Handlers walked German shepherds up and down the streets. Lights went on in the houses. A few people came out and stood on their front steps to see what the commotion was about and, as long as they were up, to have a smoke. Flashlights shone through the bushes and the windows of parked cars. Garbled voices came over the deputies' radios and went silent as quickly as they'd come. The dogs finally stopped at a pickup truck and began to bark. Underneath it lay the driver, his stomach on the asphalt.

Since he was a stocky man and since he had to keep his hands in front of him where the deputies could see them, it took some time for him to extricate himself. When finally he lay facedown on the street next to the truck, he was handcuffed and informed of his rights, and only then, as he was pulled to his feet, did anyone get a good look at him. His chin did not quite rise above the level of his shoulders, and his face was wide, the skin thick, like the skin on knees, and his eyes were small and set closely together. There was a scar above one of them. His name was Robert Corona, and he had a lengthy criminal record in Florida, ranging from robbery to possession to assault, which meant that he was familiar with the procedure, and once in handcuffs, he relaxed. He was asked how he had come into possession of Musil-Buehler's vehicle, but all he would say was that an older woman had loaned him the car. Soon he wouldn't say even that.

Deputies drove out to Anna Maria Island then, to the address where the car was registered. The house was set back in the trees, and when they knocked at the door, a tired-looking older man answered. His name was Thomas Buehler, and he was the woman's husband. He said he hadn't seen his wife in two days, and feeling like this fact required some justification, he explained that while he and his wife still officially lived together, they were no longer married in the traditional sense. They still shared their home, but she spent most of her time at her new apartment on Magnolia Avenue, with her boyfriend. What had happened, Tom asked. The deputies told him that someone had been pulled over in her car. "Well," he said. "She's dead then. She'd be dead before she let someone drive her car."

At her husband's suggestion, the deputies also stopped by her apartment and spoke with her boyfriend, but like Tom, he was unable to offer them any useful information. They'd had a falling-out two nights before, he said, and she'd left the apartment in a huff. He'd been trying to call her, but she wouldn't pick up.

Later that morning, Tom Buehler signed an affidavit stating that to his knowledge Corona at no time had permission to use the vehicle. A report was made, and shortly after, on an otherwise mild, breezy day, Sabine Musil-Buehler was officially entered into state and national databases as a missing person. It was during this time that the vehicle was processed for physical evidence. According to the probable cause affidavit:

> During processing, blood was found in several locations inside the driver and passenger compartments of the vehicle. There are several areas inside the vehicle where pieces of the seats and carpeting have been removed. The surfaces around these locations including the driver's seat belt were found to be stained with blood also. A cell phone charger was found plugged in, inside the car, but no cell phone, purse or other items belonging to Musil-Buehler were found. The trunk of the car was packed with clothing and other personal items belonging to Musil-Buehler. Due to the presence of blood and no known whereabouts for Musil-Buehler this investigation is being treated as a possible Homicide Investigation.

The sheriff made his announcement on Friday morning, the first of many announcements he would make to the public regarding Sabine Musil-Buehler. Though he refused to name any suspects, he named three persons of interest. The first was Robert Corona. The second was the woman's husband, Thomas Buehler. The final person of interest was the boyfriend, a man named William Cumber. As the sheriff ended the press conference, he asked that anyone with information relating to Sabine Musil-Buehler please contact his office, and that was how the search began.

The newspapers and the local TV stations displayed their usual knack for turning the life of a person inside out, like a pocket. The Bradenton paper found an old photo of Sabine squinting into the sun, and this was printed alongside long descriptions of Corona's criminal record. The boyfriend was quoted as saying that he loved her, and this quote was followed directly by a note that he'd recently been incarcerated for setting fire to a previous girlfriend's home. And no newspaper could help mentioning that the missing woman had shared ownership of a house and motel on Anna Maria with her husband (by then, they had begun calling him the estranged husband), the implication being that Tom Buehler stood to reap great financial gain from her disappearance.

The phone at the sheriff's office rang regularly with people offering tips, leads, and suspicions. A woman had seen Sabine at the ticket counter of the Sarasota-Bradenton International Airport, checking in for a flight to Costa Rica. She had also been seen walking west on Nebraska Avenue, holding a small purse; waiting patiently at the dentist's office; or wearing a blue fleece jumpsuit in a bar in Bradenton, looking "disheveled and upset." Or she'd been seen at a bar called Mr. Bones, with a short man with long gray hair, dressed like a "pimp"—though the witness, an amiable young woman, mentioned that she had been drunk at the time, so she couldn't be entirely sure, and in his report the interviewing detective felt "it should be noted that she was intoxicated when I was speaking with her." Sabine was in hiding. Sabine had debts. She was at the Circle K and the Salvation Army. Sabine had left a cryptic voicemail on a friend's phone. Sabine was being held captive in a house with black-and-white linoleum floors. Someone was expecting a message from the beyond, which would be received telepathically via Sabine's pet parrot, and she would be in touch when it arrived. One woman said she'd found bones in the sand and carefully relocated them to the top of a dune where Chilson Avenue met the beach. A deputy rushed to the location, but Chilson Avenue was not a through street; it did not meet the beach.

Standing on a dune, he called the woman back. "Chilson Avenue doesn't meet the beach," he said. "The *bones* are on the *dunes*," she said. "The *bones* are on the *dunes*. Anyone can find them."

THAT FIRST MORNING back in Florida, feeling drowsy after my late-night stroll along Fourteenth, I pulled a collared shirt over my head, debated at some length between dress shoes and flip-flops, and finally crossed the patio of the motel and went to speak with Tom Buehler. Before the disappearance of his wife, he had been generally regarded on the island as a friendly and self-effacing member of the community, an earnest small-business owner, and a hard worker, though his businesses had occasionally struggled. But of the three men, he was the only one who had anything like a motive for committing the crime. His marriage to Sabine, like the three before it, had long been defunct, and some said that he had been duped into the arrangement in the first place. He stood to take full ownership of their house on Anna Maria, as well as the motel, and it was eventually revealed that he was the beneficiary of not one but two life insurance policies. Many recalled his anger when he'd discovered Bill and Sabine's affair, and the mutual enmity between husband and boyfriend was well known (in his interviews with the sheriff's office, he rarely used the man's name, preferring the epithet *scumbag*). More than anyone, he was positioned to benefit from her disappearance, and he was the only person, it seemed, who had any reason to want her gone.

But when I arrived at the office, the small man I found there with glasses on his nose did not look the part of the murderer. His neck was short and his ears were wide, and a fine gray stubble covered the back half of his head. Though his body, bent over a computer keyboard, was tense, the roundness of his face seemed to predispose it to smile, and when I walked in, he did just that and asked what he could do for me.

I introduced myself and explained, haltingly, that I was hoping to talk to him about his wife, that I wanted to write a story about the disappearance, nothing sensationalized, and even as I spoke, a look of bodily horror overtook him. He had stood when I told him my name, and now, as I continued to speak, rambling at this point, about how this story might be important, how I hoped to tell it in a considerate manner, he was backing away from the counter, his arms tucked around his chest and the skin tight around his eyes. Those eyes were of a distinctly pale blue, and they watched my mouth with mounting tension as it formed yet another syllable and another. "I just want to hear what—"

He threw up his hands, and those eyes began to dart, looking first at the floor, then the ceiling, then back to me, then at his hands, which he now held clenched before him. "I'm not talking to reporters anymore," he said.

"I'm not a reporter," I said. "I'm a graduate student in a writing program."

Here his posture eased slightly. "A student." He looked at me again—I had chosen flip-flops—and seemed to consider this plausible. "Where?"

"Iowa."

"That's a long way."

"It is."

Now he shifted his weight from foot to foot, looking past me as if hoping someone else might walk in the door and rescue him from this situation. "A student. I don't know. Can I think about it? Can I think about it and get back to you?"

I wrote my cell phone number on the back of a brochure, and with this in his hand, he seemed at last to have regained his equilibrium.

"There's one other thing," I said. His face paled, and again he raised his eyes to me. "I stayed here last night, and I was hoping to stay another five nights. But I only have two hundred fifty dollars."

"Five more nights?" Relieved to return to the customary relationship of motel owner and motel guest, or maybe only thankful to have something specific to do, he sat again at the computer, his fingers pecking rapidly at the keyboard. "Five nights." He hemmed and clicked, hemmed and clicked. "You'd have to pay up front, and I couldn't give you a kitchenette. I just couldn't."

"I don't plan to cook."

"All right, I think we can work something out." His face turned to the computer, and he began rapidly typing. "So you're in college," he said. "They should make kids in college learn about sales. Why don't they?" Here he paused and looked at me as if truly perplexed. "Life is sales. It's about convincing other people that they want what you want. It's about convincing other people to give you . . ." He paused, seeming to lose his way in the thicket of his own speech. "To give you what they want." He laid a receipt out on the counter between us. "With tax it's an even two hundred eighty."

I bit my lip. "I only have two hundred fifty."

He grimaced, turned back to the keyboard again and printed another receipt, this one for $250.82. I had the feeling, as I counted the bills out of my wallet and pulled the coins out of my pocket, that those cents represented to him a matter of principle and pride, that it wasn't really a sale unless I parted with something I had intended to keep.

WITH MY BILL settled, I hurried up the street to the island coffee shop. Racks of sunglasses stood on the counter, alongside bowls of sand dollars and bric-a-brac and curios and postcards of otters (*You Otter Be Here*). All the panels on the drop ceiling had been removed, and a variety of sea paraphernalia had been wedged in the four-square metal structure: buoys, starfish, flip-flops, surfboards, pieces of driftwood, red and blue and green glass balls. A sense of nostalgia predominated, not for the Gulf specifically but for some broad idea of the sea. And beneath a shelf of faux driftwood, on a long green velvet divan, a reporter from the island newspaper was waiting for me. It had been her article, the keenness of her details—the old woman threatening to leave the island, the heavy gear of the firefighters, the anguish of a motel guest who had left his Labrador in his room—that had caused me to undertake this trip, and I was surprised to find a diminutive woman with a pageboy haircut and a ball cap. She seemed prepared at any moment to dissolve into a crowd, and she spoke so quietly as she introduced herself that I could hardly make out her name. She tilted her head as I asked her about the case, and after thinking a moment, she spoke with exactingly enunciated syllables.

"Nobody knows what to think. Some people think her husband killed her. Some think it was her boyfriend. Some think it was the man driving her car."

"Corona?"

"He seems like pretty bad news—lots of arrests—but the sheriff's office seems pretty sure it wasn't him. Just a case of the wrong place at the wrong time."

"Have you spoken to the husband or the boyfriend?"

"Tom Buehler—he's the husband, you know that—he certainly has the motive, as I'm sure you've heard. They co-owned their properties, and there was a life insurance policy, two hundred fifty thousand dollars, I think. But everyone who knows him doesn't seem to think he could have done it."

"He seems like a good guy?"

"A good guy, yes, but also a little"—she scouted around for the right word—"scattered, I guess. Has trouble finishing projects, can't stay focused. Not the type to dispose of a body without a trace. And then he has an alibi, too. He was at a party the night she disappeared." She looked momentarily uncomfortable. "I actually was at that party, too. It's not a large island."

"I tried to talk to Tom this morning. He didn't seem too excited."

"He won't talk to anyone anymore. I think he didn't like the way the whole thing was played up in the news. Bill, though, that's the boyfriend, he actually asked me to interview him. He's . . ." She paused again to look for the appropriate description. "He's funny. Just before Christmas, he called me on my cell phone and asked me to meet him on the beach. He said he had very important information to discuss. I'd heard he was losing it. He was sleeping in the toolshed of an abandoned motel on Fourteenth Street, right across from the bar where her car was abandoned, if you can believe it. Anyway, when I got there, he seemed pretty drunk. He hadn't shaved. He had this backpack that he carried around with him everywhere, and he just held this backpack on his lap and smoked one cigarette after another."

"What was the important information?"

"That she was still alive. He was sure of it, and he was going to find her. He kept saying that he loved her, he missed her."

"Did he say anything else?"

"He said he was going to stay on the island, he had to find her, he had to see it resolved." One of her thin eyebrows arched. "Two days later, he took off. They found him up in Ocala and put him right back in prison for violating his parole."

"I guess you don't think she's still alive."

"It's weird," she said. "It's just I've never seen anything quite like this case."

"How do you mean?"

"You've got grand theft auto, driving without a license, resisting arrest, arson, violation of parole, maybe insurance fraud." She listed each item off on her fingers. "But there's just no body. It's six crimes in search of a murder."

Having watched the journalist disappear down the street on an old bicycle, I walked around the corner and stood in front of the apartment building where Sabine Musil-Buehler had lived with William Cumber. It was a modest structure, pink beneath a high turquoise sky, and it had a modest patio and a half dozen parking spots along the road. A car with Ontario plates sat out front, and on a concrete bench a woman leaned over her knees painting her toenails. This was the last place anyone had seen Sabine Musil-Buehler alive, and I wished that my vision could penetrate not only into the building's rooms but also into its past.

When I turned back, I was confronted by a bank of newspaper machines, each of which depicted, in various photographs, the face of Sabine Musil-Buehler, and the reality of this undertaking,

the fact that somewhere a woman's body lay hidden, a fact that
until that moment had seemed quite far from me, suddenly became quite real. As I climbed back into the stifling cabin of my
station wagon, I felt much as that deputy must have felt, atop a
dune in the middle of the night looking for bones, having arrived
somewhere he never expected to be with directions he now knew,
in their very premise, to be false.

I HAVE BEEN trying for some time to understand the atmosphere that pervaded that first return to Florida. The dread that
was eventually to accompany these southern sojourns had not yet
fully unwound in me, and instead, on the surface, I felt the vaca-
tioner's sense of being merely adrift. I'd prepared for myself a busy
schedule—phone calls and lunch meetings and appointments at
the office of the clerk of court—but despite the activity ahead, a
feeling of idleness predominated.

Perhaps this is only a feature of that part of Florida, where so
many of the residents measure their days in rounds of golf and
glasses of chardonnay, but it seems to me now that the morbid nature of the project threw its shadow across everything. In the men
and women crowded along a darkly varnished bar, in the rows
of identical pastel homes, in a misspelling in the newspaper or a
soda bottle in the gutter, I thought I perceived the symptoms of a
universal decay, among which the disappearance of a woman was
only the most striking example.

No vacationers had fled the island fearing for their lives. In
fact, the reverse was the case. A great many people followed the
events with keen interest (though not always with great attention
to detail). If I went out one morning for eggs Benedict, someone

was sure to be talking about "that man Corvona" or "the million in life insurance," and it was not uncommon for a car to drive slowly past the burned portion of the motel. When the deputies set out a perimeter on the beach and began looking for clues, a crowd materialized in minutes. A wife called her husband at the hotel where he was sunbathing, then reported that he was on his way over. Two women canceled their lunch plans and set up their folding chairs nearby. One nodded at the detectives and said, "Let's go to lunch when they go to lunch."

When I began asking questions about the missing woman in a bar one afternoon, an emaciated man with a busted flip-flop cornered me beside the jukebox to tell me he knew for a fact that Sabine Musil-Buehler was a lesbian and her boyfriend, Bill Cumber, was gay. "What do you think goes on in prison, man? They *turn* you," he said. He knew all of this because he had been undercover on the island for the last thirty years—"C-I-A," he said, pronouncing the letters with a pause between each—investigating the gay conspiracy, and did I know that 99 percent of the people on the island were homosexuals? He laughed. "You didn't expect that, did you? Now you'll be a little more careful about who you talk to." Then a tremor passed through his frame. He looked at me again—I was wearing a lavender shirt—and his eyes hooded, and he disappeared.

I mention this all by way of illustrating the degree to which, in the span of a few months, Sabine had already become part of people's thinking. In disappearing, she became the property of the public imagination, and the only thing uniting the disparate pieces of information was that each revealed an insecurity of the person offering it. Some of the more romantic souls believed all of it was

fake, she'd returned to her native country of Germany or fled far-
ther south, perhaps to Cuba. A few thought she'd been wrapped in
garbage bags and sunk in one of the island's canals. The wealthy
assumed a violent boyfriend had killed her in a crime of passion,
while those who lived in the apartment blocks off Fourteenth had
no doubt it was a calculated murder-for-money scheme, master-
minded by a greedy husband. I, too, engaged in that madness of
speculation, perhaps more so than anyone, as I'd begun to track
down and interview those who had known her. It seemed no matter where I went, I ran into some minor acquaintance with a scrap
of information that they found crucial to understanding Sabine.
"If she saw a child and an animal lying in the street," one friend
told me, "and they were both about to be hit by a car, Sabine would
save the animal." Someone said she'd cried at her birthday party
when a balloon floated away.

In my motel room, I kept a stack of note cards, and each piece
of data I collected, I wrote on one of these cards. At night, I laid
them out on my bed, arranging and rearranging them. I was convinced that somewhere in this pile of anecdotes and photographs
and recollections was the vital clue, the detail that would make
everything slide into place, and as I began to assemble all the information I'd gathered into an idea of a woman, I imagined myself
at the head of a troupe of deputies and detectives, leading us all
inexorably in the direction of Sabine Musil-Buehler.

SHE WAS A thin woman, slightly above middle height,
with a blunt nose and dark-blue eyes set wide on her face. Sun
and age had begun to deteriorate her appearance. She still had the
smooth gait of youth, the same narrowing of the gaze and quick,

sharp voice, but the line of her jaw had softened and her smile seemed weighed down. She was concerned about her appearance, some thought overly so. She had seen an orthodontist about having her teeth straightened, and she'd begun to work with a personal trainer. She changed her hair more often than was usual for a woman of her age; she'd worn it long, wavy, and blond, but shortly before she disappeared, she cut it shoulder-length and dyed it silver.

She was born Sabine Musil in 1960 in Montabaur, West Germany, and throughout her life she retained the singsongy cadence and the soft *r* that so defines the natives of that region. Her father had been a lieutenant in the Luftwaffe during World War II. After the war, failing to find work as a wood-carver, he'd become a tax consultant. Her parents' marriage was not a happy one, and they separated when she was still young. We like to think that life's challenges serve to draw us closer to each other, but as often as not they reveal only that we were never as close as we'd imagined. The divorce blew Sabine's family to pieces as simply as a bomb. Her brothers were much older and had borne witness to the dissolution of the parents' relationship. When the mother and father separated at last, it was a welcome end to what had been a painful and embarrassing drama. They felt relieved of some unnameable obligation to one another. From that point on, she lived with her mother and her brothers in a working-class suburb of the city.

Sabine's childhood was a difficult and lonely one. When her mother was out, she was left in the care of her brothers, which is to say she was left in her own care. There were the facts of any child's life: she attended birthday parties, watched television, ran through rainstorms. If she kept a diary, there is no record of it.

Where her thoughts went at night, what nightmares haunted her, what games she played to pass the time, and what books she hid in the feathery dust beneath her bed, whether she heard the locomotives in the rail yard—the sequence of clanks, one rapidly following another, as each car lurched forward behind the one preceding it and a train churned slowly off into the night: these are questions for which there are no answers. One item alone seems to shed light on her childhood. On her eighteenth birthday, she received one present, from herself—her first official act upon emancipation—a tubal ligation, thus ensuring that no child of her own would ever live through a youth such as hers.

Perhaps it was also these experiences that drove her to the aseptic, impersonal world of hotels. Certain depths of misery do seem impossible in a place designed for brief tenancies, and she seemed to find shelter in the life of lobbies, elevators, and en suite baths. She worked her first jobs at hotels around Stuttgart, eventually taking a degree in hospitality, becoming a manager, and at last, finding work as a travel agent. All of her life slowly tilted in the direction of vacations, and it was not so much of a surprise that she finally took one herself. A friend had recommended a little island on the Gulf side of Florida.

She knew on her first visit to Anna Maria that she would live there, and on her second visit, she found a job as a manager at a hotel. In those first dizzy days of coming to know a place and its people, life went quickly. She built sandcastles, she drank wine at sunset, she adopted a parrot, and though she was afraid of the dark, she sometimes swam at night.

One day at work, a friend introduced her to Tom Buehler. It was not a lovely surname, but two weeks later, by the action of a single hyphen, it was appended to her own. She had gained citizenship in the union, and it was sometimes speculated that perhaps her intent in wedding Tom had not been entirely romantic. If this was the case, it did not prevent them from developing other aspects of their relationship; not long after, they became business partners, buying a motel from a retired couple and throwing themselves into its operation. In a picture from that time, she is sitting in an office before a computer. Her face washed in its blue light, the rest of the room dark around her, she seems to convey the middle-aged steadfastness of a woman whose secrets, like her passions, are modest and inconsequential, a woman who, despite the bustle of life, has found some comfort. I would have said, had I stumbled on this photograph in another context, that her life appeared too boring for anything bad to happen.

If any equilibrium had existed, however, it was upset by the entrance of William Cumber. He was younger than Sabine and handsome. He'd worked at the motel briefly a few years before, and when he'd gone to prison on an arson charge, he'd written to Tom asking for money to buy a few necessities: toothpaste, deodorant, soap, anything. Tom hadn't responded, but Sabine had, and over time she and Cumber struck up a correspondence. Eventually, she would bring him out to the motel each Saturday for his furlough, and not long after this, she confided to her friends, they had become romantically involved. Tom soon discovered them, and asking only that they not pursue the affair at the motel, he forced Sabine to find somewhere else to carry on their relationship. By the time Cumber was paroled on the first of September 2008, she'd rented a small apartment near the tip of the island for them to share.

Many of her friends wondered what exactly she was thinking; they worried she had fallen into the relationship too fast. Though she had always been a relatively carefree woman, she seemed to have lost some sense of herself around him. At the bar two blocks from their apartment, she was often seen sitting on his lap, her arms wrapped around his neck in a teenaged caricature of love. Two of her friends had tried to speak with her about it, but they hadn't known what to say.

What did this all mean? Nothing, or almost nothing. These fragments hardly constituted a person. They were ideas of Sabine, not Sabine herself, and it occasionally seemed like people were looking for someone else entirely.

The sheriff's office made no greater headway than those of us who tried to wring our answers from parrots and photographs. The likelihood of finding a missing person drops rapidly with each passing hour. When the sheriff made his first announcement on Friday morning, it had been roughly sixty hours since anyone had seen Sabine Musil-Buehler, and they had little idea where or how to begin looking. They examined her home computer for clues but found only "nude digital images of her alleged boyfriend." On the motel's public computer, there was "an abundance of male pornography and images of vehicles" but little else. All day Friday and through the weekend, deputies scoured the county, trying to turn up any information they could. They searched the motel. They searched the house she'd shared with her husband and the apartment she'd shared with her boyfriend. They spoke with friends and family, and they took photographs and buccal swabs. They investigated patterns of trampled grass and confiscated, as though at random, a couch, a pair of shoes, an empty bottle of pinot grigio.

Having no other evidence to go on, they spent a day walking cadaver dogs through an undeveloped lot on the mainland. The records from that period are filled with the notation *possible blood*, but it usually wasn't.

When the motel caught fire twelve days after her disappearance, it seemed as though they might be closing in, but this trail also went cold quickly. They still hoped to discover her body at least, and by January, the detectives had turned their sights to a stretch of beach on Anna Maria. There, with the help of a backhoe, a professor of archaeology, and a cadaver dog named Dexter, they'd begun digging, and it was in this position that I first found them: a number of men looking down thoughtfully at a large hole. At a cost of tens of thousands of dollars, they had so far managed to uncover a child's plastic shovel and a lone leopard-print flip-flop. (*The K-9 unit alerted to the presence of protein, but it was determined to be unrelated to the current investigation.*) As a deputy glumly admitted to the gathered crowd of tourists, the backhoe laboring behind him, it was like the woman just dropped off the face of the earth.

4: The Dark Side and the Other Side

THAT WEEK ON ANNA Maria passed quickly. I met with the woman who'd been the first on the scene of the fire. I left polite voicemails for the media representative of the Manatee County Sheriff's Office, asking to be put in touch with the investigating detectives. Over large plastic cups of lemonade, in the living rooms of Sabine's friends, I looked at scrapbook after scrapbook, and afterward, in my car, I had hushed phone conversations with those who wouldn't meet me in person.

"Tom asked me not to talk about this, but just because he's innocent doesn't mean he can tell me who to talk to."

"Listen, what you have to realize is that Sabine had a dark side. There was a dark side to her, and then there was the other side. She wrote a one-woman play, and in the end, the woman dies."

"After Sabine disappeared, I drove over to the apartment where she was living with that Bill Cumber, and I told him to his face, I said, 'I know you killed her.'"

Only on my last day did I hear from Tom. It was dinnertime, and the sounds in the background gave the feeling of a meal in the final stages of preparation. He seemed to have spent some time preparing what he was about to say, and he ran through it almost without pausing for breath. "Cutter, it's Tom Buehler, I thought it over. I thought it over, and I'm not going to speak with you. I just can't. I'm sorry, I just can't." Before I could say a thing, he'd hung up.

By that time, I had already packed my things. Tom had long since ceased to feature in the story as I understood it. Robert Corona, too, I'd dispensed with. He was still in the county jail at that time, awaiting trial for the theft of the convertible. But by then, he'd become a comic side note to the homicide investigation. Shortly after he told detectives that an older white woman had loaned him the car, they returned to question him a second time. They asked him again what had happened, and he repeated his story. Then another detective came to visit him, this one older, with ears that stuck straight out from the sides of his head, and so tall he had to duck when entering the room. This detective asked him to repeat his story one more time, and when Corona had finished, the detective asked his permission to take a buccal swab so they could test his DNA, thanked him, and got up to leave. Then he turned back. He wanted Robert to know that this was a very serious matter. The woman who owned the car had probably been murdered, and this testimony made him the last person to see her alive. "Are you serious?" Corona said. He recanted everything within the hour. He'd been looking for change in the cars parked on Fourteenth, he said then, and there was this white convertible. It was unlocked. The keys were in the ignition. He was just going to take it for a joyride.

It was around ten o'clock at night when I left Anna Maria and began driving north. That whole winter had been particularly cold for Florida, and that night by chance was the coldest. On the radio, the broadcasts were interrupted by updates from local meteorologists. As I drove past one dark field after another, they broke in to announce that it was now thirty-four degrees, to interview worried farmers, to discuss the crystallization of water, and to remind listeners that more than a few hours at the freezing point would destroy the state's strawberry crop. Sometime deep in the night, they somberly announced it was now freezing in Florida, and I pulled to the side of the road to try to sleep. But it was a hopeless project in the cold. I lay there half-awake and listened to the hiss of the irrigating machines as they crawled across the fields, spraying the strawberries in a vain attempt to save them, and a little before dawn, I put the car back in gear and continued north, toward Chipley.

Chipley, Florida, way up in the Panhandle, near Tallahassee, was a long drive from Anna Maria, a drive made longer by the fact that the only reason to go there was the penitentiary. Eventually, the fields gave onto low hills of thin, sickly pine, through which the road was cut as though with a single stroke. In that blue haze before dawn, everything loomed up, appeared for a moment, and just as quickly dissolved back into the fog: a trailer half-hidden in the trees; a town composed of a church and a bar, facing off across

the highway; culverts full of tires and refrigerators; abandoned developments; bleached subdivision flags; and, just before the turnoff, the body of a black dog on the shoulder of the road, curled up
like it had just then gone to sleep.

I'd sent a note to William Cumber a few weeks earlier, asking
whether I could visit him, and within days, a large white envelope
had arrived with a correctional facility stamp on it.

Mr. Cutter,

I'm in receipt of your letter. I'm not going to write much because I'm not trusting you all that well right now. Here's the form
that you need to fill out. Make sure you fill it out completely. Also
attach a little piece of paper at the upper left hand corner of the
application with the name, tape it on.

So until we meet be good!

William J. Cumber

P.S. Write me back also to let me know you mailed it.

Another letter followed quickly after:

Mr. Wood,

I am curious about you. I keep wondering if you're just out
to stab me in my back like the reporters and the media did. My
girlfriend's disappearance is a complete enigma to everyone. Especially me and those closest to her are troubled deeply on her
vanishing.

If we're to start an interview through letters than someone
has to ask the first question. I guess it will be me. What is your
true objective? I'm hoping that it's to put the truth out there.

You know it kills me knowing the reason why I got all this time. I really think the judicial system sucks. The fact of the matter is I'm innocent of having anything to do with her missing status.

Whatever she's doing, wherever she's at, if she's still alive, she really needs to let people know what's up. You know if you come to see me your gonna have to spend at least two days with me. There's gonna be a lot of confusing statements made and I'm gonna have to explain them.

Did you know that the motel that her and her husband Tom owned caught on fire 10 days after she was reported missing? Of course I was prime suspect number one. That too they can't charge me with because I have an alibi.

It's hard to write about it. So I'm gonna go. Till I hear from you again.

Sincerely,
William J. Cumber

P.S. I'm sorry if my writing is hard to read. You're not some kind of investigative reporter are you?

And a day later:

Mr. Wood,

Also I've done a little research on you. I know you have a brother and sister that write also. Carol and Stuart. I couldn't find any books by you though.

Sincerely,
William J. Cumber

I couldn't say why he finally decided to speak with me. The life of a prisoner is defined so completely by its unrelenting monotony that possibly, debating between boredom and me, he chose me. I had the sense, too, that as he'd once fixated on Sabine, thinking she could rescue him from his circumstances, he'd now turned this focus on his new correspondent. And I felt myself already being drawn into the unfamiliar logic of Cumber's thoughts. Unable to resist the impulse, I had looked up Carol and Stuart. About the work of Stuart Woods—born 1938, author of seemingly a thousand novels, from *Hot Mahogany* to *Mounting Fears*—one could only say, as a reviewer for the *Houston Chronicle* had, "I try to put Woods's books down and I can't." Carol Wood, working in the medical romance vein, was the author of *The Honourable Doctor*, *The Patient Doctor*, and *The Irresistible Doctor*, along with *Back in Her Bed*, the *Rogue Vet* series, and *An Old-Fashioned Practice*. She believed, according to the brief biography on her publisher's website, in "the recuperative nature of love."

The prison was set back well into the woods, and the trees had been cleared in a circle around it to the distance of a rifle shot. The buildings were low and gray, their windows few and small, and around them ran two chain-link fences, one just a little taller than a man with upstretched arms and, two paces beyond it, another twice as tall. Every few hundred feet was a cement guard tower, and encircling everything—the tops and corners of the fences, the sides of the towers, the roofs of the buildings—were long, looping thickets of concertina wire. A single white van ran a circuit around the complex, paused before the gate for exactly forty-five seconds, and went around again.

About a month after the fire at the motel, William Cumber

decided to leave Florida. He also headed north, but outside Ocala the Florida Highway Patrol pulled him over for driving with expired tags, and having no license, he was summarily taken into custody. It was late, and nothing might have come of this if at some point during the booking process he hadn't mentioned that he was being framed for murder in Manatee County. One jurisdiction called another. Leaving the county violated the terms of the parole agreement for his arson conviction, and he was quickly brought before a judge. These violations are commonplace—someone is unable to pay a fine or forgets to call his parole officer—and the punishment is usually a return to prison for a period of a month or two. But hoping to buy time for the ongoing homicide investigation, the attorney for the state pushed for the maximum penalty, and Cumber received it. He was ultimately ordered to serve out the full remainder of his sentence, thirteen and a half years.

By then, his picture had been printed plenty of times in the paper: a strong jaw, broad shoulders, and thick brown hair. Parts of his criminal record had been printed, as well. I'd had the tentative impression that he was equally handsome and violent, and I was more than a little surprised to find a small, listless man waiting for me in the visitors' room. His head had been shaved; his skin was gray and ashy. All the color had been wrung out of his eyes, and although his face was bloated, it was obvious that beneath his blue uniform, there was little to him. He shuffled across the floor to meet me, shook my hand weakly, and we sat. He looked at me out of the corner of his eye.

"I thought you'd be older," he said, and when I shrugged in reply, he stood up. "You hungry?"

Visiting hours ran eight to two. We sat with a pile of microwavable sandwiches and pastries between us, and for the first three of those hours, he spoke cautiously, looking up every so often between bites. He was in for an arson in Bradenton, he told me, not the one at the motel. The detectives had tricked him into confessing to that crime, he said, and now, he was careful about who he did and didn't talk to.

But over the course of that first morning, he gave me a rough chronology of his life. He'd been born in the coal town of Ashtabula, Ohio, well after the mines had been worked out. His father had been a mechanic, an immensely strong man, capable of picking up an engine block in his arms, and it was in this posture that he was photographed by an investigator from the insurance company and prosecuted for fraud. His mother had been a pleasant woman, whose affairs led to the end of the marriage. Cumber didn't know what they were doing now. He'd heard they were still alive, but he had no wish to see them. His childhood lay scattered across the East Coast and included cameos by exasperated relations, well-meaning foster parents, and a German stepmother of singular cruelty. At fourteen, he was in foster care, and at fifteen, a juvenile detention facility. At eighteen, he married and had a son, and not long after this, convinced that his wife was cheating on him, he'd broken into someone else's home. He wasn't trying to steal anything, he said; it was just the only way he knew to keep from killing his wife. He wanted to be locked up, and the state of Ohio obliged him. From eighteen to twenty-six, the prime of his life, he'd been in prison.

Time was dim, he regularly said. He did not like to think back on the past, and because of this, he had difficulty remembering it. He'd be forty before too long. Since that first incarceration, he had not spent any considerable period outside of prison. He did not mention that even those brief intervals of liberty had been crowded with minor altercations and arrests, fines, warrants, and restitution. Nor did he describe the detailed record of charges and arrests I was to discover later. They spanned two decades and a thousand miles: trespass, disorderly conduct, driving without a license, driving while intoxicated (level 5), speeding, possession of stolen property, possession of marijuana, possession of paraphernalia, driving while license revoked, driving while impaired, driving while intoxicated (level 2), open container, breaking and entering, larceny, assault, simple assault, battery of a law enforcement officer, cultivation of marijuana, arson, failure to wear a seat belt, fishing without a license.

"In here, man, I'm fine," he said. "No problems. A model prisoner. Out there?" He shook his head.

We didn't come around to the topic of Sabine until the afternoon. She deserved to be found, I told him, and he looked at me for a long time.

"You say her name like she did," he said. "*Suh-BEE-nuh.*" He licked his fingers. "The detectives say *suh-BEEN.*" He reached for another pastry. "We don't get real food in here. You play cards?"

THE ONSET OF their affair was rapid and poorly concealed, and in short order, they were discovered by Sabine's husband in one of the motel's suites. At the time, according to Cumber, that marriage was just a piece of paper filed at the courthouse, and her husband was angry less about the affair than the fact that they'd chosen to pursue it at the motel. Tom said if they wanted to continue seeing each other, they do it elsewhere, and so by the time Bill was paroled on the first of September, Sabine had rented an apartment for them out at the northern end of Anna Maria. She furnished and painted it, and when he got out she threw him a welcome home party. The relationship wasn't perfect, he said, but whose was. Tom tried to come between them, Bill said. That was the hardest part. Sometimes they argued about it, and then she would leave the apartment and spend the night at the home she still shared with Tom. Without a driver's license or a car, Bill felt trapped on the island at times, totally dependent on her. But those disagreements were the exception, not the rule. He and Sabine loved each other. They took bike rides, went out for dinner, walked on the beach at dusk. He gave up smoking for her. They had planned to go to Germany together.

"What about that night?" I said. "What did you do that last night?"

"Just regular boring stuff," he said. "We watched TV."

At one point, he'd gone outside to smoke a cigarette. He'd quit for her birthday, but he didn't think she'd know if he snuck one. The quarrel that followed was unhappy but typical. She grabbed her keys and drove away. That was it. As he'd told investigators again and again, he tried to contact her but he hadn't seen her since. He thought she might be still alive. She'd always talked about running away somewhere, and he hoped she had. He just wished she'd let someone know.

By this time many of the other visitors had left. The guards were preparing to close the room.

"What about the blood?" I said. "Aren't you worried about her?"

"Heck yeah, I'm worried about her, man." He picked up the deck of cards and shuffled it. "I loved her, man. I still love her."

We stood and shook hands.

"Hey," he said. "Real quick, and I don't mean any disrespect. But there's nothing to do here. I mean it gets *boring.* Do you think if I sent you some titles of books you'd be able to help me out?"

5: Impulses Diverted

MY DEPARTURE FROM FLORIDA after this interview bore some resemblance to a man disappearing into a crevasse. One moment, I was sitting in the parking lot of the prison listening to my messages; the next second, one could just make out the whinny of a loose steering belt in the distance as the station wagon banked a curve and headed north. The reason for this hurry was quite simple. There had been three messages on my phone when I left the prison: the first, from Forrest, saying that if I was free he'd be happy to show me sandcastle pictures whenever was convenient—he was available all week; the second, from my mother, wondering if they'd found that motel woman yet—she hoped I was having fun; the last, from Erin, saying that she couldn't stop thinking about me—she wanted to meet.

I had to teach my first class of the semester in Iowa in about thirty-six hours. I spread the atlas out on the passenger-side seat. It was possible. If we met halfway, we could share four or five hours before I needed to turn west. I called her back, and as our rendezvous point, we selected a motel, the very name of which—the Lynnette—seemed to promise some indefinable intrigue. I was on the highway even before we'd said goodbye.

I feel I should note here that when I considered the coming hours at the Lynnette, all thoughts of William Cumber and Sabine Musil-Buehler were swept from my mind by my lewd and far more immediate hopes for the near future. I was a young man, it will be remembered. I lived alone and drove a station wagon. As I sped north, I did not think of the prison I'd left behind but of the motel that lay ahead. I imagined swaying pines in the parking lot, a shag rug in the office. The room would contain a television in its own faux-oak cupboard and a mustard-colored couch onto which we would tumble in a confusion of lips and limbs. It is important to also note, though, that tied up in those imaginings was some embryonic vision of what it would be like to be around Erin. I imagined, for instance, that I would read aloud to her from the works of Sir Thomas Browne, that we would walk along a leafy country road, that she would shower while I lay in bed, listening to the water run. The motel would have an attached miniature golf course, where, between wholesome romps, we would putt a little. With the pines of Georgia blurring outside my window, I was already developing some idea, however unrealistic, of what life would be like in her company.

Shortly after noon, on a rural valley highway deep in Appalachia, I slipped through the opposing traffic and wheeled the

Taurus into the empty gravel parking lot of the Lynnette. I had driven the night through without stopping, and I was by that moment so involved in my own thoughts that the full visual impact of the motel did not at first strike me. It was not until I reached the double plexiglass window of the office, yellowed by age and crazed with minuscule lines, its corners begrimed, not until having plaintively rung the brass bell for some minutes, that I turned around and began to absorb the surroundings. The motel formed a narrow horseshoe, the top of the U facing the road and a fallow field, the U's bottom concealing—I could just hear its gurgle—a brook, where one could imagine a few abandoned grocery carts upended on the rocks or the kerchiefed remains of a missing Boy Scout. The building itself, though to call it a building implies a uniformity of form and structure so markedly absent, reminded me of those false-front Western sets, the worn mishmash of facades ready at any moment to collapse into their original timbers. I heard a man groan, and in a dim doorway at the back of the office, a large figure appeared. In his general features, I recognized him instantly as a fixture from the sub shops of my youth: faded blue jeans, a sleeveless undershirt, a gelatinous belly straining a leather belt, which creaked as he approached.

"Do you have a room available?"

He sucked on a thick finger and squinted at a wall of beaverboard, on which every room key hung.

"What's available?" he shouted, and again in that dim rectangle at the back of the office, a shape appeared, a pale woman, pushing before her a vast beach-ball pregnancy; she could only be the eponymous Lynnette. She leaned against the jamb, eyeing me from behind a tuberous nose, and my febrile brain immediately imagined the man, fresh from some lawn-mower repair, pawing at her in the vacant rooms of the motel.

"Give him twelve," she said, and receded quickly into the dark, where, a moment later, a baby cried.

He hunted around in a pile of magazines, finally locating his guest ledger, and he began to take down my information, writing with concentration. As I watched the pen move deliberately across the page, my thoughts turned to the passing minutes, the sun overhead, and the effect it might be having on the champagne, the box of chocolates, and the bulk carton of condoms sitting on my passenger seat.

"Method of payment?" he said, and he looked up as a dark-blue sedan whipped into the lot. The shock to my system must have registered clearly on my face. He laid on me a grin. "With you?"

She wore a jean skirt, and a tight shirt, striped blue and white. She was jacketless and jaunty as she stepped out of the car into the January air. I nodded, and he flipped back a page in his ledger. From the back room, the hoarse voice of the woman shouted, "Give him number eight!"

ERIN AND I soon stood side by side in the doorway of our room as upon a great precipice. The fragrance of some common deodorant drifted off her, and the boisterous smell of peppermint gum. In other circumstances, that scent would have palled, but it delighted me now with its portents of unabashed kissing. Number eight had no mustard-colored sofa, no microwave, not even a bulky black television on which only *Full House* played. The walls were paneled in pine. On the ceiling, a fan swung slowly, circulating a clear ammoniac air. On one side of the room hung a painting of irises, and beneath it was a queen bed, strikingly white, its sheets tucked and folded crisply.

"Champagne?" I said, crossing the floor and standing against the far wall.

"Please." She lay back on the bed. "Pretty comfy."

The cork ricocheted around the room and lost itself in some dark corner.

"To freedom," I said, sitting beside her again and holding out two plastic cups.

"To today."

I threw back my glass and refilled it. "So how was your drive?"

She sat up then, pulled the cup from my fingers with a few soothing sounds, and pulled me down to the mattress with her in such a way that my mouth landed atop hers, and in near silence, some pleasant moments passed.

The champagne, the chocolates, and the condoms all evidenced a very distinct, if clichéd, sense of purpose, and while I wasn't entirely certain of Erin's plans, I thought I at least knew my own mind. And yet after that kiss, as we lay on the bed at the Lynnette, outlined by a broad panel of afternoon light, when she pulled away and held herself at arm's length, regarding my eyes for a sign of the thoughts behind them, my constitution underwent some drastic and sheepish alteration. Prior to this moment, I had flirted, dined, dated, and even slept with women, and I had some sense of the trajectory of things. So I was all the more disturbed then by this lack not of desire but of will. I could not bring myself to reach out, to make the next gesture that would indicate my own interest in the project at hand. It was as if I'd forgotten how the machinery worked.

I cast about desperately, as one does under extremities of duress, for some external cause. My mind sprang from one thought to the next without logic or pattern. I watched the fan spinning above us and thought perhaps there was a chill in the room dampening my desires, or, catching sight of a small vent positioned high on one of the walls, I imagined the owners of the motel, secreted away in their voyeurs' loft, siphoning the ardor from our own tepid endeavors to fuel their own wild and shameless acts. I felt suddenly exhausted, and I thought that certainly if I hadn't driven all night, if I hadn't spent the past hours counting down the miles and watching the eyes of does swim up like flecks of neon in the headlights, if I hadn't spent the past days looking for a woman who was at that very moment probably moldering in a shallow unmarked grave, then perhaps I would have been able to do as I'd wanted, to take her in my arms and declare her mine. It occurred to me that if I could simply focus, simply keep my mind on one thing—the tip of her nose, for instance, or a certain knot in the pine paneling— then perhaps I would be able, by latching on to this physical detail, to regain control of my thoughts. But no sooner had I fixed my eyes on the knot of wood than I thought it looked like the profile of Sabine Musil-Buehler, and I recalled the interview of the day before, the warmth of the pastries in their plastic packaging, the slow action of Bill Cumber's jaw as he chewed, and the whitening of his knuckles around the edge of the table as he spoke about that night: *I loved her, man. I still love her.*

Perhaps thirty seconds had passed. Erin still lay at arm's length, the side of her head against the pillow. A strand of hair had fallen down across her cheek, and taking it between my two fingers, I pushed it back from her face and tucked it behind one ear, and she, as she often had when we were younger, arched first one eyebrow and then the other. Then, seeing that she couldn't elicit even a smile from me, she moved her forehead so that her brows waggled together in a single fluid wave. And because I had no words to explain what was actually occurring in my mind, I smiled and introduced some other topic of conversation.

It hardly matters what I said, since my only reason for speaking was to make the hours pass as quickly as possible. I recall some observations about the weather, an explanation of the near loss of the Floridian strawberry crop, the recitation of a sermon I'd chanced across on the radio about the sins of Onan. I spoke at some length about Sabine Musil-Buehler, about the fire at the motel, and about the strange man I'd just met, who I thought might have committed murder, and I watched as she listened, first with interest, then bemusement, then confusion, and finally, propping her head up on one hand, with resignation.

I'd first met Erin in seventh grade, the year that Katie Briggs got pregnant and Katie Karlson broke both legs jumping from a tree house, and Katie Tedesco, whom all the boys dreamed to fondle, kissed Travis Podolski for an hour and a half in the back of a rented van on the way home from a birthday party at the skating rink. This was also the year, due to some glitch in the primordial computer system then creating middle schoolers' schedules, that I was unable to eat lunch at the normal hour with my peers; and so I faced the prospect of a year of dining alone, my only company being the lunchroom monitor, a student teacher in algebra.

I had eaten perhaps three of these solemn repasts when Erin appeared. She had not yet attained the height that would eventually disqualify her from serious gymnastics competition, and so to accommodate her rigorous schedule of practices, she too had been exiled to my lonely lunch island. Of that first day, I remember only that I had a pork sandwich and grapes, and that Erin, to my amazement, after extracting, arranging, and eating one bagged lunch from her backpack, pulled out a second one and repeated the process exactly, a strange Nietzschean reiteration that she was to continue every single day and that she explained to me, without the slightest embarrassment, was a gymnast's caloric necessity.

Looking now at a photograph of the two of us from that time, it is clear to me that puberty, not wanting to launch children too soon into their careers of love, provides its own prophylactic, and I have difficulty believing that either of us, even in the most deranged states of mind, could have been attracted to the other. My laissez-faire approach to personal hygiene had resulted in a marked slouch, grimy fingernails, and a large blond Afro in the mold of Carlos Valderrama. Erin possessed the broad shoulders and calloused hands of an uneven bars specialist, and the athlete's preoccupation with sweatpants and sweatshirts, and beneath that coarse gray fabric, her body was but a cruel rumor. In addition to this, her physical development had proceeded unevenly, an affliction of gymnasts and nongymnasts alike, and her petite frame had been far outpaced by her generous and regal nose.

But such prolonged contact with a member of the opposite sex during this testosteronally precarious interval was bound to have an effect, and from time to time, I imagined a day before school when one of our disgruntled classmates would fire a bullet into a crowd of his peers, a bullet that I would intercept just before it struck Erin's heart, whereupon swooning in her arms, I would make some sort of confession and we would kiss. We exchanged notes almost daily, notes in which I tried to make known to her the feelings I myself hardly realized I possessed. They nearly always featured a series of multiple-choice questions, this form being the most familiar to middle schoolers. By such obtuse and limited means, I wooed:

If it was midnight, and raining, and the only warmth you could find in all the land was a hot tub full of lukewarm green Jell-O, who would you be most horrified to discover already in said tub:

A. Mrs. Dieffenderf

B. Horace Wells

C. Mr. Angley

D. Me

My confused attempts at courting that year were made even more hesitant by the recent death of my grandmother. The victim of some unnamed illness, she had spent my childhood in a state of near total catatonia, seated statue-like in the corner of the kitchen, only her eyes moving to follow me as I crossed the room. It was not until her death that spring that it occurred to me there may have been no physical illness, or rather I overheard two relatives surmising as much, speaking in low tones behind the arborvitae at the funeral parlor about the cruelty to which my grandfather had subjected her—never meanness outright but a gradual and cumulative disdain, under the force of which she had slowly worn away until now she was finally gone. At the time, I did not feel any anger toward my grandfather about how her life had ended. Nor was I disturbed by his speedy reentry into the world of dating. I only resented that I was obliged each Friday to put on a collared shirt and to go out for dinner with my parents, my grandfather, and a new date.

My grandfather's approach to courting bore no small resemblance to the blitzkrieg that we were then learning about in school. As Rommel sped across the sands of Africa, swift, ruthless, unrelenting, Judge Wood sought to overwhelm and exhaust the stock of local widows by the application of pure speed. No woman, provided she was single, was spared in this assault. An entire bridge club was invited to dinner, one by one, as was my maternal grandmother. One week, with a horror surpassed only by her own, I found Mrs. Dieffenderf seated at the table, still dressed in the purple sneakers and purple sweater that were for her a sort of uniform, but doused now in a gardenia perfume.

Some of these women devoted themselves to performing for the family, querying me on my extracurricular activities or starting some other line of inquiry fated to peter out in my trailing whispers. Others devoted themselves to my grandfather, placing a hand on his arm at every comment that even lightly grazed the realm of witticism. Still others, thrust unfortunately into a role for which life had left them singularly unprepared, sealed up as primly as a clam and stared at the half-drunk glass of chardonnay on which their lips had left a smudged pink stain. The sharp falsity of laughter, the practiced gesture of the hand placed on the arm: that these were somehow related to the orgiastic pulse of middle school, or to the dark-eyed girl with whom I ate lunch, was deeply unsettling.

Having watched with Erin the theatrical gropings of two of our classmates backstage during a play rehearsal, and then turning immediately to the fluttering laughter of an octogenarian as my grandfather held her eyes with his own, I felt that whatever love was, it was laced from end to end with error and self-deception. It was not that I was determined to avoid the mistakes of my grandparents or my peers. I was simply terrified of the thing, had always been terrified, and it was this terror, resurrected by my own attempts to learn about a missing woman in Florida, that returned to me as Erin and I lay together at the Lynnette.

In the end, perhaps it didn't matter that our first time alone together was spent in such a stagnant manner. Everything might have gone on just the same if we'd found some sort of rapture that day. But what might otherwise have passed quickly was drawn out by that long and celibate afternoon, establishing a tentative cadence, and in this way we began our relationship. As Freud would have been happy to note, the sexual impulse cannot be stifled; it can only be diverted. And even before parting, we'd made plans to see each other again.

WITHIN DAYS OF returning to Iowa, I'd received a letter from Chipley. In a rushed dark pencil script, it read as follows:

Cutter

The detectives came to see me again. They said that they would try to get me 20 years for the murder of Sabine. I told them that I'm not giving up 20 years of my life for something that I didn't do. They say that they have alot of D.N.A. evidence on me. When I tell them of course that they would have alot of D.N.A. evidence on me. Why, because we lived together. They can't seem to understand. I know that they have blood in the apartment and in the car. But that blood that's in the apartment must of gotten there when she would peel fruit and cut herself from time to time. I'm through talking about it. It just bothers me. Well I'm gonna get going for now. Catch ya later.

Bill

P.S. I wanted to let you know the books I wanted you to send when you have the ability to. I have just finished Stephanie Meyers New Moon (Good stuff). I would like to read the next book that's in the Series. It's called Eclipse. This Next Book reveals unanswered questions etc. where New Moon left off. Right now I'm finishing up the 3rd book in The Game of Thrones. A Clash of Kings. Pretty good stuff although it can be a little confusing.

P.P.S. Who knows they could be reading my letter prior to mailing them. I wouldn't put it past them.

Sitting in my turret with this note before me, I saw the fire at the motel as clearly as if I stood before it. The streams of water wended between my feet, the smell of smoke lay heavily on my clothes, and the sky brooded above my head, and with what even then I thought of as a kind of Faulknerian detachment, I felt the meaning of this image unspooling inside me. Just as certain pieces by Bach were constructed as puzzle boxes, the first bars a cipher from which the rest of the composition could be deduced, I found in this fiery motel everything necessary to write. I saw Tom, rushing this way and that in pursuit of his own thoughts; Sabine, careering subject of her own whims, adopting toward the men in her life an attitude similar to the one she took with pets; and Bill, the rambling lover of mystery novels, who'd been unable to escape the violence of his own past. And in that fire at the motel I saw the ultimate finale.

I wasn't sure what part Bill had played in Sabine's disappearance, but I had no doubt that he'd set fire to the motel. The sheriff's office had confiscated his shoes and a blue Bic lighter for chemical analysis, and they considered his alibi weak. He'd been sitting on a nearby dock, he claimed. It made no sense that he would have set the fire. There was nothing to gain from it, and with all the attention on the case, the blaze only served to throw greater suspicion on him. It was precisely the senselessness of this act that drew me. It wasn't a story I wanted to write as much as an essay on the urge to destroy, and I thought that if I could but arrange the broader history of fire in just the right way, it would culminate in the moment, frank and revelatory, when Bill struck a lighter.

As winter eased into spring, I fixed myself intently on my task. I rose at ten or eleven, made a cup of tea, read a few of Orwell's essays or a passage from *Swann's Way*. Then, almost bursting with purpose, I threw my satchel over my shoulder, vaulted down the front steps, and marched through the snow to the blank and monolithic library. There, I absorbed myself in a near-fanatical research into fire, accumulating one instance after another from the historical record as the volumes multiplied around me in the fungal air of the reading room. Occasionally, needing to stretch my legs, I would set off for some far unknown corner of the building, half-blind in the storm of my thoughts but also almost painfully perceptive, as if simply to look at a thing was to rub myself against it. The whispers of two students in the stacks skittered like oil across the hot pan of my brain. The scent of a tangerine tormented me, and I envisioned it resting peeled in the fragrant palm of some undiscoverable undergraduate, she herself sitting no doubt on the wide inner sill of a chilly window annotating Keats's letters, waiting already, without even realizing it, for the feverish tome I would soon unleash upon the world. Such sensations and imaginations sent me back to my desk, on my way inevitably passing by an aged scholar, bent down to the very rim of the table, the thick lenses of his glasses nearly grazing the page, or one of the true lunatics, hissing curses at unknown figures from behind an upside-down volume of *Calvin and Hobbes*. In my rush to return to work, I had only a flicker of compassion for these men. Never did it occur to me that forty or so years earlier, they too might have embarked, like myself, on their "research."

Later, I'd adjourn to a nearby bar to drink a whiskey and sink slowly, as if entering a familiar puddle, into the conversations of writers and drunks. Under the Bunsen-like influence of the liquor, the first sentences would begin to form themselves, slowly, the words tumbling till they notched into place, and by the time the sky had darkened, I was already ensconced in my turret. The work did not come quickly or easily. I was not content with a mere story, after all, or even with a philosophical explanation of arson; having examined them, I found the psychological and sociological perspectives ultimately unsatisfying. How could a discussion of emotional triads and psychotic markers fully encompass the sequence of events that would lead a man to set fire to the motel of a woman he loved?

I had never entirely left behind my sixth-grade penchant for tragedy and disaster. Laboring to achieve the weighty tone that would both intimidate and seduce my reader, I set to writing my brief history of the various fires that from time to time had consumed some portion of humanity. I had (I thought of my collection then even as a boy might) all the best fires. There was the Great Fire of London, so well described by Pepys, after which the city had been built again almost as if a dream made real by the great architect Wren. There was the burning of Rome, with its monkeys screeching across the roofs, as well as the burning of the Library of Alexandria and the legendary tracts therein. I had the Great Chicago Fire of 1871 and the destruction of Lisbon in 1755, a disaster of incomparably comprehensive proportions, first in that it overlapped with a tsunami and an earthquake, and second in that it brought to an end the world-enwrapping Portuguese empire; it was a fire, too, that carried with it my essay's first hints of psychological import, for the king had been caused such trauma by the event that he would never again consent to live in a solid building and resided the remainder of his life with his court in an endlessly shifting city of tents.

I was careful to also make note even of the smaller conflagrations, those for instance that consumed but a single soul, like the burning of the heretic Jan Hus, whose pyre would not catch until an old ragwoman, hoping to be helpful, offered the soldiers in charge her bundle of dry twigs. And I was in particular struck by the near-total destruction of Hamburg by the Allies in July of 1943, and by the description of the ensuing firestorm, which was said to breathe its oxygen with such force that people fleeing were sucked back bodily into the inferno, and birds in the outlying districts of the city dropped dead from asphyxiation. I fastened especially on the description of a single man, a young German seated on his balcony a few miles from the blaze. He watched the firestorm with, he was surprised to realize, a steadily increasing enthusiasm. "I had only one wish," he wrote in his journal. "Let it get really bad."

From this giddy jaunt across the annals of death and destruction, I was diverted only by the overwhelming need, late in the night, to sleep, and waking up the following morning, I repeated the procedure almost point for point. There were just two disturbances of this monastic schedule. The first was the occasional letter from Bill Cumber. I had recently sent him a copy of Stephen King's *Needful Things*.

> Cutter,
>
> What I'm about to say I don't want you to take the wrong way but before I do I want to let you know that I am very thankful for all your help and support and I'm not ever going to look a gift horse in the mouth but I thought I sent you a list of authors and the titles of their books that I was interested in reading. Did you not ask me to provide it to you so you could send what interested me. I do like Stephen King but I had hopes on continuing the Stephanie Meyers series. When I got the S.K. book last night I had already been reading Stephanie Meyers second book New Moon. The next is Eclipse.

The second disturbance was the arrival, every so often, of the documents I'd requested from the Manatee County Clerk of Court. It was in one of these that I first encountered the defense Bill had given when he'd been brought before a judge for his violation of parole, a long, rambling monologue that stretched on for pages in the court reporter's transcription. "If I start talking in riddles," he'd begun, "and stuff like that or whatever because, like I told you before, sometimes my thoughts get ahead of me and I try—and I don't want to get ahead of my thoughts by talking too fast, so if I come to that point, stop me, please." Then he'd gone on.

I'm sorry to have to speak on this but it has to do with Tom was in control. He would—and Sabine abided by it, you know, she was like, well—how did she put it? Gosh, I can't remember. It's an agreement, yeah, an arrangement that we've made. I'm like, okay, you guys made an arrangement, well, the arrangement is I can't be at the motel, I can't be at your house, I can't do this, I can't do that, you know, whatever is going on, you know, I felt secluded. I couldn't do anything. So we would have little arguments here and there about it. But then, you know, things started getting real stressful for us. And I had quit smoking for her on her birthday. Well, I started smoking again and she didn't like that. All right? Smoking, boom, we get in an argument, she takes off. Now after that, she's missing. Some three days later, I find out she's missing. All right? And after that, who do they want to decapitate over the situation? Me. Because they brought up all my prison arrests, my conviction, whatever, my whole police record, my whole life history damn near was spread around out there like creamy peanut butter over freshly toasted bread, you know, just to single me out. Okay? Then the motel catches on fire. And who do they want to blame? Me. Because I just got out on parole from the arson charge.

Okay? But I was somewhere else when this fire started. But apparently, the police didn't want to believe that. They call my alibi weak. I can't help that she left the house. I can't help that. I don't know what's going on when she leaves the place, you know . . . I have no . . . I'm not . . . it's just so . . . confusing.

He concluded his defense some pages later. "You know," he'd said. "I tried my darnedest."

6: The Worse Truth

IT WILL SEEM HASTY if I say that at this point Erin and I moved in together, but this feeling of haste lies in part in the fact that I must condense here some months of blissful courting. We spent that spring fleshing out the story of our own affair with all the sorts of petting and chirping and planning—we would grow tomatoes, we would visit Arizona—that are so joyous to those who perform them and so onerous to those who must witness them. But I was the one who nudged the relationship along. I suggested we meet one weekend in Chicago. I booked the hotel; I made the dinner reservations. In the morning, I went out and got us coffee, and I led her through the Art Institute, always a half step ahead.

After, in our room, where everything—floors, ceiling, walls, trim—was painted in the same eggshell white, and where the only window looked out on a brown brick wall, so that there was no way to tell which way we faced, I lay in bed watching through the bathroom door as she readied herself for dinner.

"Do you always wear makeup?" I said.

"When I'm going out."

"What kinds?"

"Mascara," she said. "Sometimes lipstick."

"What else?"

"Undereye concealer," she said. "But that's a secret."

I was in the doorway of the bathroom now, watching her as she leaned in close to the mirror. "You don't need it," I said.

"That's what all men say. You don't know what I look like without it."

"Don't wear the lipstick, at least," I said.

There was a short step up from the bedroom to the bathroom—they must have laid new plumbing, I thought—and she came over to me and stood on that step, so that our eyes were nearly level. And knowing that it was an unwise suggestion, knowing, too, that I didn't yet mean it, I said I thought she should move to Iowa.

She did not say yes then. Beyond smiling, she did not react at all. She went back to the sink and finished putting on her mascara. She put her lipstick away in her purse and began to gather her clothes, putting on first underwear, then bra, then a blue dress, which, standing again before the mirror, she pulled at here and there adjusting it into place. I lay back on the bed, enjoying this ritual of getting ready, which I had complicated just slightly, and as she brushed her hair, I looked forward to dinner.

I don't think I made the suggestion out of love—we had hardly begun to know each other—but neither do I think it was made on entirely faulty premises. At least in part, it was an experiment. I wanted to see what she would say, how it would affect the evening, the weekend, the days after, the forked path of our two lives, and having made a habit of considering and reconsidering every act in my life, I wanted to see how it felt to be the impetuous one. Perhaps, too, I still wanted to make up in some way for that afternoon at the motel. There was something protective in the act. It seemed to me that by behaving rashly, by behaving unlike myself, I was shielded not only from accountability but also from the distress if she said no. I was half joking, I told myself. Tomorrow, I could just as easily suggest the very opposite. It was her fault if she took me seriously today. There was even, in my rush to yoke our lives together, a first element of, if not cruelty, some precursor of that emotion. I knew that I was moving ahead of my own feelings, and I knew that I was suggesting something unwise for her, nearly impossible—asking her to throw over her life for my own, leave behind work, friends, the streets she walked down and the windows she looked out of, the whole structure of her days. But I wanted this. I wanted to possess the figure in the mirror, to call up her face as simply as pulling a glass from the cupboard. I wanted the path of her life to bend to my own.

We walked to dinner arm in arm, dressed in clothes that neither of us felt comfortable wearing. My tie kept blowing over my shoulder, and above the scrape of my shoes, the staccato tap of her heels echoed in the empty street. The restaurant was in a district of warehouses and auto garages, the lights and the din of conversation perceptible even from far away. We sat out on the sidewalk still hardly speaking, while the dishes came out one by one:

whitefish, meatballs in a spiced ragu, a roasted hen. The day had worn on us, we were tired and hungry, and it was only as the food arrived that we again picked up our conversation. As each new dish was settled onto the table, I warmed a little more to my own proposal.

"What's crazy," I said, "is the idea of living a thousand miles apart. It doesn't make sense. Either we're going to wait around a few years and move in together anyway, or we're going to call the whole thing off. We might as well figure it out now."

"Don't be silly," she said. "That's not how it works."

"Quick is the way to do it," I said. "Like taking off a Band-Aid."

"Then move in with *me*."

"Let's not get off topic," I said, and refilled our glasses with wine. "We could even buy a house."

There is a fundamental difficulty in describing the attributes of one's beloved in that first flush of love, let alone in picking out which among them is the *prima mobilia* of one's feelings, and this is that one's delight infuses all aspects—not only of the beloved, but also of the scenery surrounding her—with a luminous charm. The whiteness of the tablecloth, the couple nearby in the midst of some marital dispute, the anxiety of the young waitress, who, walking toward the bar, repeated solemnly to herself, "Gin, up, dry, twist, gin, up, dry, twist": these things in their fitting loveliness were indistinguishable from the woman who sat across the table from me, lost in thought above the menu, one hand of its own accord reaching up to twirl a strand of brown hair.

My attention did emerge from time to time to settle on this or that detail—her careful manner with a salad fork, or how, with a few words, she put the waitress at ease—but these details were picked out almost entirely at random, and I might as easily have found some other gesture just as darling. And the worse truth is that of the things I noticed about her, the majority were forgotten as quickly as they came, and the few that remain with me have survived not by virtue of the particular allure they held that evening but because in the time that followed I returned to dwell on them. That night they were only gestures, and their beauty lay in the fact that I hardly knew what they might mean.

In any case, she didn't say yes that night. In fact, I can't recall whether she ever said yes, either because she didn't or because I never waited to hear it. And though it was hasty, it seems it was necessarily so, since compared to the reality of cohabitation, in which one sees the shared mornings stretched out, as in a funhouse mirror, ad infinitum, everything previous appears rushed.

JUST NORTH OF Iowa City, Dodge Street left the highway, passed a cemetery and a dairy collective, made a bend at a pair of cedars, and swept downhill into town. The house we rented was behind those cedars. On the side nearer to civilization sat a stumpy building, shingled in lime-green asphalt and occupied by a hermit, who had lived there with his mother since childhood and had continued living there since her death in 1996 (he stood in the front yard narrating this as we carried our belongings up the stairs); he now spent much of his time collecting and organizing the "perfectly good" towels left behind by sorority sisters at the end of each semester. On the other side sat an electrical transformer. It gave forth a low ruminative thrum, occasionally crackling maliciously. From the parking lot across the street, the house looked much like the house in the painting *American Gothic*, but as one drew closer, this resemblance began to diminish. The porch had been replaced at some point with sheets of plywood, which bowed ominously under one's weight, and when the rental agent stopped by to say hello, the front railing detached in her hand and clattered to the pavement.

But it seemed to us on that day entirely lovely. There were two apartments, ours on the first level and another, empty, on the second, and in our unit two bright rooms with oak floors and deep bay windows took up the front of the house. In the back, a large kitchen and a bedroom looked out into a woodsy gulch. No matter that a Ford Ranger sat on blocks on the adjoining property, its cab stacked to the brim with neatly folded towels. No matter that the second floor was vacant because a writing student had hanged herself there (scorned by her professor lover, it was said). Erin and I had secured our life together. I saw my desk before one of those bay windows, and myself seated at it, my cup of coffee beside me, the typewriter clanking querulously as I banged out my opus, and I was untroubled that in this imagined scene, flooded with light, Erin was but a dim figure somewhere in the other room.

That afternoon, as we closed the doors on the emptied moving van, it was as if we were sealing off a former portion of our lives, as if that van contained all the uncertainty that had previously animated our experiences of love. There were to be no more chance brushings of a hand across a knee, no more wondering what such incidental contact might prefigure, no more dallying at the end of a night, no more hesitation at all. And the closing of the door to her apartment, the soft clicking of the lock in its catch: these were gone, as were the three steps down to the pavement and the long blocks stretching away from her house, which I walked with her in

mind, or maybe without thinking of her at all, thinking of a story
I might write sometime, or only looking for the right word to describe the green of magnolia leaves at night and wondering if in
five years or ten I'd remember this moment.

Instead of that expectancy, of conjecturing what the night
might hold, there was on that first evening only a vacuum. In the
apartment, boxes stood in columns around the rooms, books lay
across the floor, a dozen glasses sat on the counter without anywhere to go. We set to work cutting through tape and unpacking.
For some reason—maybe we simply hadn't yet acquired the habit—
neither of us turned on a light when the sun set, and the rooms
were already dark when we realized we had stopped making progress. We found a set of sheets in a trunk and, standing on opposite
sides of the mattress, made the bed.

"Does it feel stuffy in here?" I said.

"I was just going to ask you that."

And with the window open and the sounds of the night filling the room—cicada calls, an owl, an eighteen-wheeler coasting
downhill—we fell asleep.

WE WENT TOGETHER, our first outing as roommates, to
a barbecue. The event took place in a backyard that was reached
through a narrow passage between house and fence. Even as we
moved out of this cramped darkness into the grassy lawn beyond,
much overhung with oaks, the texture of the air attained that elec-
tric sizzle of long-cooped brains let loose. In the alley at the yard's
far end, two people stood beside a grill while a third sent a wag-
gling stream of lighter fluid into it, and in the distance between,
at varying degrees of discomfort from the large blue bucket of ice

and beer, the writing students stood in little groups, the burble of their conversations rising and falling.

"No," an elfin woman was saying, looking up into the branches of the oaks. "His prose isn't exactly *static*. It just suffers from a certain . . . lividity of detail."

"I like the dialogue," someone murmured.

"It may be the overuse of metaphor," said the first.

"Schizophrenia," said another, though whether to the group or to herself remained unclear.

"You know that anecdote about Dickens and Dostoyevsky," said a man whose chest hair sprouted thickly from his shirt. "Young Dostoyevsky goes to visit Dickens, and Dickens says to him, 'It's like I have these two voices in my head, and they can't agree.' And Dostoyevsky says, 'Only two?'" The man laughed so uproariously at his own joke that two more newcomers were drawn into the circle, and as he began the anecdote again, the woman closest to us, dressed head to toe in black, turned to Erin.

"What do you write?"

"Oh, I'm not a writer."

"That is so refreshing," said the woman, and turned away.

If we are smart, of course, we recognize the difference between a person's popularity and their worthiness of love, but who is immune to the desire to see the things one cherishes celebrated at large. Through the eyes of others, everything that had so disarmed me about Erin was inverted. I wanted her to divulge some of her unprepossessing genius, to reveal herself as the woman who had studied Titian's brushstrokes and yet saw wolves in *Beowulf.* I wanted her to show that lexicon so deeply affected by the terminology of gymnastics that she still described getting off the couch as dismounting. I wanted her to offer some rebuttal to the woman who had shown her such marked disinterest, but the conversation had moved on. A man was talking about a sailboat, a gorgeous sailboat that he was going to restore, had already basically begun to restore, a perfect little sailboat on which he would give us all rides.

"The wind, the sun," he said. "At night, the stars."

"I was on a sailboat in Alaska," said Erin. "The nights were so still, and there were so many stars."

The hostess, her face encircled by ringlets, laid a hand on Erin's arm. "Did you see the foot on the treadle of the loom?"

"No," said Erin. "But I saw some sharks."

Undoubtedly, she was coming to see me differently, as well. My ability to define uncommon words, my sardonic commentating, my infatuation with cynical frames of mind, and my covetous collection of anecdotes (later that night I would transcribe the story of Dickens and Dostoyevsky): these attributes played well in certain crowds, but seen against the uniform background of writers' neuroses, they were drained of any individuality or interest. Now having seen the type, Erin must have begun, with some satisfaction, to tick off all the ways I fit it, and in my tennis shoes and baggy jeans, standing beside a man whose arm was sleeved in a tattoo of Whitman, I was not even a particularly exemplary specimen.

In the alley, they were still trying to light the grill. I began to pull Erin away, but we were intercepted by another young couple—she, dressed in a draping sweater, he, in a light green jacket. They had returned only minutes ago from an excursion to the mall.

"Harrowing," she said, her chin lowered to indicate seriousness. "I nearly had an attack."

"I looked over," the man said, "and she was literally swaying."

"All those fat people, all that cheap pizza, and the *candle stores.*"

"I dragged her out to the car, maxed out the AC, and pumped NPR."

Previously, Erin and I would have gone our own ways, and there we could have built up again, in privacy, some idea of who the other was, but now we only walked back slowly in the direction of our house.

Saying that one is happy is a little like saying one isn't afraid: less convincing the more one insists upon it. And yet when I think of the rudimentary life we assembled in Iowa, I feel with some conviction, much as Bill Cumber must have felt, that we were happy. We fixed the railing, planted basil, looked up whether the violet berries on the bush out back were edible or poison. On brilliant, cool mornings, we walked the city, looking at the houses we passed, each in its turn, and discussing what we did and didn't like—swimming pools, shade trees, screened-in porches— mentally sketching out the blueprint for some nonexistent home. And when a bank of clouds blew across the plains and the sirens went off downtown, we sat out on our front porch and watched the wind whip the trees into a frenzy. In one of the storms that summer, a tornado swept through a Scout camp during its emergency preparedness seminar. We both thought it was funny, but we never spoke about it to anyone but each other. It was one of a thousand things, a hundred thousand, that existed between us and us alone; our life, in this way, was woven of these mundane moments. If a tornado had touched down on our house and wiped us both from the earth, it would have taken with it more than our individual lives; it would have taken with it this shared existence. When I think of that house now, in fact, it is as if a tornado had destroyed it. Picking up a plate that once sat in those cupboards, I am struck at once by how unrecoverable that life is, how much more I might have appreciated it.

In place of the uncertainty that had lent excitement to our early days, our two routines slowly took their positions. In the morning, I watched her lean against the end of the bed as she pulled on her jeans. I stood at the stove, flipping eggs, while she measured out the morning's coffee, or she cooked the eggs while I got the toaster off the high shelf. I had loved to listen to her bathing, had been almost unable to tear myself from the sound, but now, already wrapped in a towel I waited for her to finish her shower. I looked at the mail, I got out the clothes I would wear, or I sat with a book at my desk. When she was finished, I entered the bathroom, hung my towel on its hook beside hers, and, before I began to wash myself, dragged a finger across the tiles on the wall, gathering the long brown hairs strewn across its surface into a spiderlike knot.

In all my fantasizing, I had entirely failed to imagine this reality, this glomming together of two lives that changes both and leaves neither intact, and I was startled to realize how poorly our existences overlapped. We both woke at the same time, but she was out of bed in an instant while I preferred to loiter in the sheets and let the day come gradually. The moment she woke, she wanted to turn on all the lights in the house—she couldn't see, she said, and it was depressing. Even on the gloomier days, I preferred the gray light that came in through the windows to the yellow glow of the bulbs. She had already been at work for hours when I at last took my post at the library, and at five o'clock, when she was pouring herself exactly half a beer, I was just beginning to write. She would have liked to spend our evenings together, to go out for dinner, to see a movie, but by then I was too engrossed in my work to be distracted. By the time I switched off the light at my desk, she was usually asleep.

As we tried to find some pattern to the day that suited us both, the apartment seemed to take on a life of its own—dictated by neither of us but born into being by our inability to agree or our rush to find consensus, by the fickleness of our moods or our faulty beliefs of what the other might like or tolerate. We grew geraniums. We painted the walls a pale turquoise. We hung gauzy curtains in the windows. And each of these decisions helped create a space that did not belong to either of us (she had wanted begonias; I'd wanted blinds) but was hardly ours. Certain resentments built up by necessity in this process, but they were always minor, passing, forgotten almost as quickly as they occurred. When she mentioned that the geraniums seemed to be dying from some fungus, I knew that she was really lamenting the unbought begonias, just as she knew when I asked whether she had seen a certain book, that I was actually asking whether she had moved it, accusing her really, and so it was not unreasonable for her to say in response that she had no idea, hadn't gone near my desk, hadn't touched anything. A tone of fleeting exasperation entered our voices at these times or, because we were aware of that tone, of mock exasperation, and some of these questions, asked with enough regularity, even attained the status of something like a joke. "You've been hiding my books again," I would say, but neither of us laughed.

It was very easy then, always in vanishingly small increments, to place a little more blame on the other for the disappointments and frustrations that had formerly been ours as individuals. It was easy to think, for instance, that the misplaced book was crucial to my work, absolutely necessary in fact, and as I rummaged the shelves, I found myself formulating an unspoken argument, not so much against her as against our situation. It was plainly impossible to work like this, so my thinking ran, with these interruptions and disturbances, with her looking over my shoulder or clanging pans in the kitchen, or asking whether I wanted to go for a walk. *Untenable* was a word I often thought. *This situation is untenable.* Then when the missing book was discovered, the whole thing ceased to matter. Everything was back to the way it had been before, but the word *untenable* remained.

It didn't help that my work was going poorly. My original vision had evaporated, leaving me to sift my notes in hopes of finding some clue that would lead me back in the direction of Sabine Musil-Buehler. And yet, refusing to acknowledge this fact, I pushed ever backward into the history of fire. I'd begun at that time to describe the conflagrations of prehistory, the burnings of those early human settlements with their mud-brick homes and clay idols, and I'd gone back yet deeper into the past, to fires tearing untamed across the savannas that only *Homo erectus* might have seen. I was at that time elaborating upon a certain Amazonian tribe whose creation story held that all humankind had been created in the collision of the planet with a giant flaming lump of sloth dung, and I knew even as I was writing the words *giant flaming lump of sloth dung* that I had gone irretrievably afield.

Around that time, I also began to collect stories from the

newspapers in Manatee County, ostensibly to keep in mind some
sense of the place. In reality, I was losing faith in the whole premise of human relationships, and each of these stories was part of
the evidence:

By triangulating data from a number of cell phone towers, detectives had been led to a drainage pond behind a Publix su-
permarket, where, in a number of black plastic garbage bags
stuffed into a pipe, wetsuited divers discovered the dismem-
bered remains of Susan Fast, whose stepson was arrested later
that day at the gym . . .

Hearing a commotion in the hall, Crystal Johnson stepped out
of her bedroom into a "hail of bullets," which were being exchanged by her boyfriend and three men who had entered the
wrong apartment . . .

William Howery, standing in a parking lot, holding his child,
was stabbed by a man he'd never met . . .

After the first football game of the season, a group of girls took
their friend Jasmine Thompson home, only discovering upon arriving at her house that she had been hit by a bullet during the
drive and had died without a word in the back seat . . .

The sheriff's office released the confession of 17-year-old Clifford
Davis, 303 pages in which he described the murder of his mother
and grandfather, the chronologically-organized display of his
childhood photographs around their bodies, the perturbation
he felt that afternoon because his grandfather's pacemaker continued to fire long after the man had died, and his desire to be
remembered, like Ben Franklin, Thomas Edison or Napoleon . . .

"He molested his mother's corpse," I said to Erin. "Then he went to the mall to buy some shoes."

"You don't need to tell me everything," she said.

I BEGAN TO dream of Sabine. During many of those nights, I swam with her, far out into the Gulf, where the water below was lightless and frigid, and where suddenly her hand would lock around my arm or her hair would wrap around my ankle, and I would be pulled down. Some nights, I simply shoveled sand for hours on end, and some, I fled Florida with the sound of sirens in my ears. Most often, though, I found myself in medias res in an awkward and horrifying sitcomesque situation. One night, I was hosting a cocktail party. The room was light and cheerful, and the guests had all arrived. They leaned on the kitchen counter; they milled around the dining room admiring the view. I made some witty remark in passing and crossed into the living room, only then realizing that I was using Sabine's coffin for a coffee table. How I could have overlooked it, I couldn't say. I had to do something before someone noticed, but at that moment, the coffin began to rise slowly off the floor, causing the drinks on its lid to wobble and spill. Now I darted across the room and began to lean on it, pressing it back down onto the carpet, trying all the while to make conversation, to smile, to be well liked and worthy of love and admiration.

I was woken from this dream by my phone ringing. It was daytime, and the first cars were passing down the road. Not recognizing the number, I answered just before the final ring.

"Is this Cutter?"

"Yes," I said. "Who's calling?"

"Hey, man. It's Bill. You know, Bill Cumber."

"Bill," I said. "How'd you get this number?"

"Oh, I told my attorney you and me was friends and I lost your number."

"Your attorney? That worked?"

"Listen, bro, I don't have a lot of time. Things have been tough, real tough. They came in the other day and searched my cell and put me in the hold for two weeks. And when I came out, apparently the FBI was here, asking everybody whether I had told them anything, and offering to reduce their sentences if they gave up any information. Which they didn't, because I didn't do it, and if I did, I wouldn't've told anybody here. But anyways, that's besides the point. The reason I'm calling is—"

The phone cut out. I looked at it for a long time. Then I left it by the bed and went to take a shower. When I got back, there was a message.

"Hey, man, what I was trying to say when I got cut off is that I finished *Eclipse*, so don't send that one."

SUMMER ARRIVED EARLY that year. In the sudden thrust of heat, the ginkgo trees began to drop their fruit onto the campus sidewalks, where, crushed under the flip-flopped feet of the student body, the orange berries oozed a putrescent umber liquor. There were only a few weeks left of classes, and the undergraduates, seized by the sudden panic of impending examinations, could be seen running between academic buildings, and lining up outside the registrar's office to see whether the last day to drop a class had already passed. They pored over Wikipedia. They loitered around the desk of the weary librarian in her faded Nirvana shirt, whose half-finished book, Hesse's *Siddhartha*, lay on the desk unopened.

As a graduate student fresh with ambition, I was paid to teach these young people how to write, and I had run headlong into the courageous but monosyllabic and punctuation-averse world of late-teenaged communication. The inclination to throw up one's hands was strong, and most of the young instructors had developed their own pedagogical approaches. One had his class sit in a line facing the rear wall of the room with their copies of *The Collected Poems of Emily Dickinson* while he, as if in a game of Duck, Duck, Goose, selected who was to read the next poem. Another wooed her students by using only films with sex scenes as her course texts. A third often wept. One had assembled a list of topics for his creative writing students that—due to their tendency to descend most rapidly into monotony, self-aggrandizement, and cliché—he had forbidden. The list, emblazoned on the back of his syllabus in bold, all-caps, size-forty font, eventually grew to such length that it precluded nearly all but the most esoteric ruminations, but at that time it read only:

NO DEAD GRANDPARENTS
NO VACATIONS
NO SEX

One of my students had turned in that week a story about a young man named George, and the end of George's recent relationship. As is often the case, it was based largely on the events of the student's own life, and he had inadvertently referred to the main character as Dylan, his own name. The premise of the story was simple. George/Dylan had been dating the same young woman,

Kelly, since early high school. They had both come to the university together. They had chosen to live in abutting dormitories. They had picked the same major. But the relationship soured, and George/Dylan, knowing it was the right thing to do, had broken it off. He was now seeing someone new, Brittany, who was far better in every way than Kelly had been and—here Dylan interjected to highlight a point not stated clearly in the text—"super hot." The narrator was happy now, everything was great, he had even forgiven Kelly for being "a little bit of a bitch," and—it was reading this final phrase again that something broke loose in me—he hoped she was happy.

"Do people believe this?" I said. "Do we all really believe that George wants Kelly to be happy?"

"It says so at the end of the story," said a student.

I was breathing with some force through my nose. I looked again at the line, then back at the class. Dylan sat with his legs splayed out, his face as blank and impassive as a shovel. I turned the story over and laid it facedown on my desk.

"No," I said. "No, this just isn't the way love works. You don't just stop and start loving like that. You bring all this baggage with you, whether it's your ego or your insecurities, or some weird hang-ups inherited from your parents or from your own previous relationships. You have all these expectations about how you should act and how she should act, and because of that you do fucked-up things to each other. You know that George is probably playing Brittany the songs that Kelly used to love, and Brittany's probably using the same tone of voice with him that her mom used with her dad. You're just doomed to play out the same shit again and again, and really you're just trying to use her to obscure your own unhappiness."

In the silence that followed, I heard my entire speech play again, and I was horrified not only by its autobiographical tone but also by the realization that perhaps George really did want the best for Kelly. I had the sense that the students were staring at me with some mixture of pity and disgust, but when I looked up, I found that a few had let their gaze drift out the window. One was picking at a blister on her hand. Dylan was looking at his phone beneath his desk. The student who had spoken before raised her hand again.

"It's sort of like George still likes Kelly."

After this class, I set off for home, feeling very clearly a sense of gratitude for Erin, a need to sit down and speak with her, and a certainty that whatever indifference had entered our relationship, we could dispel it by simply talking. I wanted to tell her about my students, about the various birds in the trees, about the boy I passed in an alley, fending off invisible enemies with a stick. The house was empty when I arrived. Remembering that we were expecting guests for dinner, I washed the dishes and swept and mopped. I put on water for spaghetti and stole a flower from the neighbor's garden, and all the while I was looking forward to the moment when she would come home, when I'd tell her how wrong I had been. I wiped the glass clean in the front door and tightened the screws that held the knob in place. I set the table. I dusted the ceiling fan and then the baseboard. But as the time passed, as I realized that there would be no opportunity now for my planned confession, I began to work with a different kind of urgency. When

at last she arrived, I kissed her, but I did so too insistently, knowing already what her reaction would be, wanting to cause her to
pull away.

"They're going to be here any minute, aren't they?" she said,
already passing into the next room. "Thanks for taking care of
dinner. It looks great in here."

Of the dinner itself, I recall only that the husband of her co-
worker was more handsome than I would have liked, that I thought
Erin doted upon him more than was necessary, and that at some
moment, he revealed he was from Florida.

"Cutter's writing about Florida," Erin said, leaning forward.
"Maybe you can give him the inside scoop."

Afterward, she cleared the table and swept and tidied while
I did the dishes. I had just finished the pots and pans when she
started brushing her teeth. For a moment, we stepped around each
other in the bathroom—spitting, rinsing, flossing, washing our
faces under the tap—and then she went to bed and I went and lay
down on the couch with a book. After a while, she got up again
and began turning out the lights.

"Do you mind if I turn this out?"

"I need it to read."

"I thought you were using that one."

"I'm using both."

She went back to the bedroom and lay down, but some time
later she was up again.

"Are you coming to bed?"

"Not tired," I said.

"What?"

"I'm not tired."

Much later, I awoke on the couch with the book still open in my hands. I turned off the lights and went to the bathroom in the dark, and then, being careful not to wake her, I slid very quietly into the bed we shared.

7: Before Everything That Happened Happened

THAT WEEK, BILL'S LETTERS came one after the other in rapid succession (I had stopped picking up the phone when he called), and they sat in a pile on my desk.

Cutter,

Today I tried calling you several times but no answer. If I'm starting to bother you let me know something. It's just that you're all I have out there. It's a harsh reality but it's true. Hope to hear from ya soon.

Your friend,

Bill

Cutter,

Look dude, I don't know what's up with you but you really need to stop messing with my head. I do not need the added "like I've said before" disappointments in my life. I have tried to call you <u>several</u> times but to no avail. You seem to be avoiding me. Why, I do not know. If this is what you call friendship than I can do without it. Let me know your thoughts.

Bill

P.S. If you are able to send books please remember that I like Stephanie Meyers. Why R you avoiding me?

<u>"Live Long and Prosper"</u>

Cutter,

Please believe me when I say to you that I'm thankful for everything you have done for me and also for the things which you have mentally attempted to do for me. You have put up a valiant effort trying to be my friend and I appreciate it tremendously but I must honestly say that, "like my mother, father, the judicial system and Santa Claus," that I'm tired of disappointments in my life and that's what you have turned into to me. Maybe I'm just a game to you but I'm tired of playing games. Especially when I'm the pawn. You may find it childish but to me a man has only his word that must be honored when spoken. But know this, things have really taken a positive change of direction in my life. Freedom is all I want in life now and I will achieve it.

Thanks again,
Bill

Cutter,

This is a brief message to let you know that I received the books. I really, really, really, really appreciate it. Even though they're a simple read they still have their moments of gratification. I heard about how the youngins like Twilight. There's a team Jacob and a team Edward. One is a vampire and the other a werewolf and they both love the same girl. She chooses Edward. Tough.

I need to discuss something with you. Its business oriented so do not stress the statement. I must let you know that we are allowed to have hard backs.

Later,
Bill

This last contained, folded in quarters, a pencil drawing of a teddy bear. The bear wore a drooping bow tie and held a heart from which a vine sprouted, its tendrils spreading across the page and terminating at last in smaller hearts. The bear's gaze, cast above his head, fell fondly on a short message in swooping letters: *You are my Everything.* An attached note mentioned that the picture was an example of his artwork, and would be "suitable for a mat frame."

I was sitting at my desk, looking at this drawing. I had received a message from one of the detectives investigating the case, and I was waiting for him to call back. Even so, I was startled when the phone rang.

"This is Detective Gisborne from the Manatee County Sheriff's Office, Mr. Wood. If you have a minute to talk, I just have a few questions." He didn't pause to wait for my answer. "We did a search recently of William Cumber's cell, and we found one of your letters. I just wanted to get a sense of what sort of relationship you have with Mr. Cumber."

"I'm working on a story about Sabine Musil-Buehler's disappearance," I said. "I've been conducting interviews with people who might have information relating to it, and William is one of those people."

"Would you say you and William have a good working relationship?"

I looked at the drawing in my hand. "I would say we have a good working relationship."

"Look, I'll be perfectly honest here. I don't know how familiar you are with this case, but we believe that William Cumber killed Sabine Musil-Buehler and buried her body on the beach."

It was still an active investigation, he went on, so they hadn't released much information to the public, but they had everything they needed to hand things off to the prosecutor. Along with the blood in the convertible, his DNA was on the driver's seat. They'd found blood in the apartment, too, and evidence that someone had tried to hastily clean it up. They also knew that the car had been parked by the beach the night she'd disappeared.

"That's why you started digging out there?"

"Funny story," he said. "About a month after she goes missing, one of our guys remembers he ticketed a white Pontiac out on the island that night. We look up the ticket. It's our vehicle."

"You think he was out there on the beach burying her while the car was getting ticketed?"

"The patterns of blood on the back seat and on the front seat belt indicate that a body was put in with the top down and then pulled out of the passenger side door. We think he took her somewhere where he was worried someone might see him and that's why he took her out through the door instead of putting the top down. And this indicates, we figure, she's buried out there somewhere."

Supporting this hypothesis, he told me when they first brought Cumber in for questioning, his hands were blistered, as if he'd spent the night digging. Cumber could offer no alibi for that evening, and his story had changed each time they spoke to him. He told them that he kept trying to call her after she left, but his phone records showed that wasn't true. The list of incriminating evidence went on. They had testimony from Musil-Buehler's friends describing Bill as a violent, dangerous man, and they had the record of his very public tailspin after her disappearance: stumbling drunk down streets, pawning her belongings one by one, eventually fleeing the county. The state attorney was ready to charge him with homicide first thing tomorrow morning, the detective said. They had everything they needed to make a conviction, with the exception, of course, of the obvious thing: the body of the presumed victim.

"I'd love it if we could get you down here again, talk a little more, maybe see whether we could set up a meeting with Cumber," he said. "I think you see where I'm coming from. The family would like to put this behind them."

I looked across the apartment to where Erin lay on the couch. "I've been thinking I might try to break away from Iowa at some point this summer."

"That's great. Well we'll be in touch then." I could hear the squeal of an office chair as he leaned back. "By the way, I haven't read any of your books, but my wife is a big fan, a real big fan. She can't get enough of them."

THE AFTERNOON OF my flight was sullen and wet. The men in yellow slickers outside the plane seemed to be gesturing for help. As we waited to be cleared for takeoff, I rested my head against the oval window and watched the people and long caterpillar-like vehicles hurrying across the tarmac through the beading rain. And just as they seemed to dart this way and that with no apparent reason, I began to feel my thoughts untether from their normal course and scatter across my mind. I closed my eyes, and a number of images swam before me—tigers, bedridden men, a train running through the forest—until in a moment they cohered into a dim opera house, the walls of which, covered in ranks of red velvet seats, disappeared steeply up into darkness. I was awaiting the parting of the curtain when, with a few glances right and left, I perceived that the other patrons—decked out in pearls and jewels and grosgrain finery and eagerly awaiting the performance—were corpses.

"Sabine," I said, putting my hand out to touch her arm. "I think we're at the wrong opera. This one is for dead people."

I opened my eyes. Only a second had passed since I closed them, it seemed, and I struggled momentarily to comprehend what had happened to the tarmac beyond my window and the people walking across it, all of which had been replaced by a hazy patchwork of brown and gray. When at once I realized I was seeing the earth from a height of some ten thousand feet, I was stricken by a feeling of vertigo like I had never before encountered. It was as if in a moment the ground had been pulled out from beneath me, and like a cat held aloft above the bathtub, I clawed mortally at the air, seeking to find some purchase, discovering only the sweat-shirted arm of the Iowan beside me, who smiled, waited for me to release her, and returned to her magazine.

I carried with me on that flight my collection of note cards in pale pink, yellow, and blue. Each of these cards contained some note relating to Sabine's disappearance and to my own investigation of it.

Tom Buehler: "poster child for ADHD"

on night of disappearance, Bill made Sabine a "lovely" dinner

These I laid out on the tray in front of me, and between hesitant glances out the window, I began to arrange and rearrange them, flipping some over as if playing a child's memory game, then placing some together in a stack. But I failed to make even the slightest progress during the flight. Instead I began to sense that I was being watched, noticing at last that the woman beside me whose sweatshirt was emblazoned with a large yellow hawk was now staring at the card nearest her, which read only:

patterns of blood

Then the airplane banked steeply over St. Petersburg, the light from the low sun briefly gilded the faces of the economy-class cabin, the woman turned away, and as I gathered my things, we began our descent to the runway in Tampa.

I don't recall getting off the airplane or riding the miniature train that carries passengers back and forth to the main terminal. Nor do I recall the descent to the baggage claim. I stood beside the dirty translucent flaps of the baggage chute, watching as the items of luggage, tagged and bar-coded, emerged one by one and tumbled onto the revolving track. I remember looking into the eyes of a flush-faced boy being carried by his father, who only stared back at me defiantly when I smiled. And I recall that in some far corner of the room, two pieces of unclaimed luggage circled each other endlessly on an otherwise empty track.

Only when the glass doors parted and I stepped from the air-conditioning into the tumid and oppressive atmosphere of Florida in summer did I come to myself. A number of palms rose around me and, alongside them, a few concrete pillars. Well above was the elevated road that brought cars to and from the airport. I was standing beside a cement container perhaps six or eight feet across, sparsely planted with the very same purple-and-yellow flowers that had lined the patio behind my childhood home. The combination of bright sunlight and concrete gave the terrain an over-exposed look, and indeed I had the sense that the place had been left too long in some sort of reductive chemical bath. The vertigo that I'd felt on the flight, when the land leapt out from underneath me, had been building steadily in the hours since, and as I thought of the drive out to Anna Maria, of the appointments I must keep, and of the creeping entanglement of Bill and Sabine's story with my own, a sharp nausea crept over me.

Avoiding the motel, I took a room instead that overlooked the very plot of beach where the body was believed to be buried. I changed my shirt and went to meet a reporter from the Sarasota paper on Longboat Key, an island to the south. Separated less by the narrow channel of water that lay between it and Anna Maria than by the spiritual feel of the two places, Longboat featured ten-story condos set amid tennis courts, and the grass ran off for quite a distance from the sides of the road.

When I arrived at the restaurant, I found a small woman on a high stool, dressed in chinos and a lime-green blouse, with a half-finished cosmopolitan on the table in front of her. I had requested this meeting in the hope that some of the journalistic accomplishments of this woman might rub off on me, and after exchanging a few niceties, she set her drink down precisely in the center of a maroon paper napkin and looked at me.

"So what's your angle?" she said.

"My angle?"

"I mean, no offense, but there's nothing remarkable about this story. There was a triple homicide just last night."

"I saw a few weeks ago a woman was convicted of having sex with her dog."

"A beagle, I think."

We lapsed into silence.

"I don't think I have an angle," I said finally.

By some strange turn in the conversation, we fell to talking of our families. I narrated for her the peculiar relationship of my grandparents, and she, as if confessing, began to tell me the story of her Uncle Hank, who, in the cockpit of a single-prop ten thousand feet above Missouri, had with some violence rebuffed the pilot's homosexual advance or been rebuffed in the act of his own advance. As she described in detail the contradictory testimonies of the parties involved and the web of outrage and indignation once the men returned to earth, I began to feel with more and more certainty that I had read this exact story before, in an unfinished novella by the author Barry Hannah. The reporter's story of Uncle Hank, I believe, marked the moment when the world of simple, straightforward facts began to seem like a place I no longer occupied, and I broached that idea with her.

"God," she said, and signaled to the waiter for the check. "I wish I could make it up. Then I could start to tell the truth."

By the time I returned to my room, I was nearly incapacitated by some combination of gin and despair. The idea of rising and going out to find some bit of dinner was inconceivable to me, as was the thought that in the morning I must put on fresh clothes and say hello to other human beings. Unable to sleep or to turn my thoughts to useful endeavors, I locked the door of my room, slipped the key into my pocket, and took to the beach. I quickly found myself on that plot of sand where it seemed most likely Sabine had been buried, and with my hands in my pockets, I strolled through the brush and dunes, stopping every so often, without ever really meaning to, and digging my toe down an inch or two. From time to time, I encountered an object and reached down with my hand to clear the sand from around it, inevitably unearthing a stick or a palm frond or the plastic brim of a sun visor, and at some moment, hardly thinking, I began to dig with both hands. Soon, I was clawing at the dirt. I passed through a layer of shells into a muddish stratum. The sides of the cavity began to slough off, and the hole began to fill with water. I felt certain that she was buried here, perhaps only another inch or two deeper. I was breathing heavily and flinging handfuls of muck between my legs when I realized that she actually might be, that my hand might touch bone at any moment. I froze then, and as if seeing myself suddenly from the outside, I became aware of what I was doing. I wiped my hands on my pants and hurried back to my room.

Late that night, as I drifted to sleep, I remembered something the detective had mentioned on the phone. He was describing how they'd been digging on the beach, how many tractors were running, how they'd scraped away the sand an inch at a time looking for any sign that it had been disturbed, and how they could have missed her by six inches and they'd never know. "We've got William away for thirteen years," he'd said. "But I'd like to find her before I retire."

Some time later, I was woken by the sensation that fine particles of sand were falling softly on my lips. I did not, at first, open my eyes. Instead, I kept lying there, feeling the almost impalpable cascade of sand upon my mouth. When at last I did open my eyes, Sabine's face was positioned not an inch from my own. I tried to scream, but my lips would not part. I tried to move, but she had pinned my body to the bed. Strings of wet and filthy hair hung down along my cheeks, and though my eyes were locked upon hers, I could see somehow that the door of my room was open to the night, that a sandy path led from my bed across the floor to the beach and the hole she'd crawled out of. I cannot say how long I lay there with her atop me. When at last I managed to close my eyes, the weight evaporated from me, but even then, having understood it to be a dream, I did not look to the door to see whether it was still open.

WHEN I ARRIVED at the sheriff's office the next morning, Detective Gisborne was waiting for me on the other side of the metal detector. He nodded to the deputies in the lobby, and as we took the stairs to his office, he breathed heavily through his gray mustache. Our tour of the office—a labyrinth of cubicles, from

which arose only the sound of computer keys clicking—concluded
at his own desk, with its disarray of papers and its stained coffee
cup no different from any other, except that pinned to one wall
was a mug shot of a man who looked strikingly like Santa Claus.
"Here's a sick one," Gisborne said. "His wife drowns in their pool.
He's pretty broken-up about it. We hear back from the coroner
she's got bruises all around her left ankle. He dragged her to the
bottom of the deep end and didn't let go. Guess what we call him?"

"Santa Claus?"

"Dead ringer, right?" He surveyed the room, his head and
shoulders protruding only slightly above the level of the cubicles.
"And the scary part is, he's one of us."

"Law enforcement?" I said.

"Corrections." He shrugged. "Yep, one of the good guys."

He ushered me into an empty conference room. There, sitting
at a long table, he recited again everything he'd said on the phone,
almost word for word. It was still an active investigation, so they
hadn't released much information, but they had the material they
needed to make a case—blood in the apartment, blood in the car,
the blistered hands, the phone records, the public record of him
going to pieces—everything but a body.

"Recording technology has come a long way in the past few
years," Gisborne said, leaning over the table. "We have a device
that looks just like a credit card. You can stick it right in your shirt
pocket." He took in a breath. "What if you went to see Cumber
again? Tell him you're going to write a nonfiction book about this—
excuse me, which one's made-up?"

"Fiction," I said.

"Tell him you're going to write a *fiction* book about this. You make it clear that this is a story where everything is made-up, and then you ask him if he *had* done it, where would he have put the body." He sat back again. "Do you think he'd go for that?"

THAT NIGHT IN a rented house on Anna Maria, I met with Sabine's brother. A tall, angular man, he spoke little English, and for hours we sat together at the kitchen table looking at pictures of Sabine while his wife, doing dishes at the sink, translated. He would hand me a photograph, describe what it depicted, then move to the next, describe that, then the next. *This was Sabine at a birthday party. This was when Sabine stole their grandmother's fur coat. This was Sabine with her first boyfriend.* Between these brief phrases, the silence stretched out, and soon we were looking at one picture after another, but saying nothing. When I asked him to tell me what she had been like, he seemed unable, even in his own language, to find words. As his wife offered up possible adjectives, he sat mute beside me, clenching and unclenching the muscles of his jaw.

"*Pünktlich*," he finally said, and before his wife could translate, he spoke again, with precision. "She was punctual."

It wasn't until we were saying goodbye that he offered up a final adjective, a quick series of guttural sounds that I couldn't understand.

"He says Sabine was joyful," his wife said. He immediately put his hand on her shoulder, and they talked for a moment in German, both shaking their heads.

"He says I mistranslated," said the wife. "She was materialistic."

After that long and silent evening, I couldn't bear the idea of returning to the beach to sit alone in my room, so I drove the back streets west of Bradenton. I looked at the houses as they drifted by, and when I found myself inevitably in a cul-de-sac, I spun the rental car in a wide arc and kept driving. Erin called, but I couldn't bring myself to focus on the conversation, which seemed to me to be nothing more than a rehashing of our respective days. At some point, I pulled up in front of a mint-green house on a treeless corner lot and parked the car. I'd found the address in an old file at the county clerk's office. It was the house where Bill Cumber had lived when, as a younger man, he'd first moved to Florida.

"Is there something you'd rather talk about?" Erin said, but I couldn't think of anything.

THE LONG, PANTING drive to Punta Gorda followed one of those roads that seem, impossibly, to go on perfectly flat and perfectly straight forever, with here and there a turnoff for a used-car lot or a used-truck lot or for another flat, straight road. At last, a small sign appeared, reading OIL WELL ROAD, and I swung onto a gravel lane, bordered on the left by a line of scraggly trees and a soybean field, and on the right by a broad pasture of freshly mown thatch grass. Three horses grazed almost in the shadow of the razor-wire fence and the squat concrete building behind it.

Bill had been transferred to a new facility, and this prison provided a waiting area for visitors outside the main entrance: a few metal picnic tables bolted to a cement pad, and a hut containing a restroom. When I arrived, a number of others were already waiting: an old man in a dusty white cowboy hat, a mother and her round-faced little boy with a tuna sandwich. As the sun climbed the sky, my skin began to sizzle lightly beneath my clothes, and my shirt clung to my sides. Still more arrived: an ancient grandparent, wrinkled and sexless; a young Latina woman in a skintight dress the color of a daffodil, who, when told by the guards that her clothing did not meet the length requirement, unearthed a cell phone from some hidden crevice and made a call: *"Mami, no me dejan entrar . . . Sí, por mi ropa. Sí."* Large black flies with metallic green eyes tacked out of the shadow of the guard station, landed on a glistening neck or arm, exacted their due salt, and dissolved again into the boiling heat. And out of the restroom, a great blue heron emerged to steal between the tables, chasing in slow motion the pudge-faced boy with his sandwich. At last, a guard stepped out and gestured to us to come.

Compared to the chaotic and brusque intake in Chipley, the process in Punta Gorda was a competent and sensitive affair. After passing through a metal detector, I was buzzed into a frigid room, where I handed an officer my keys and belt to be placed in a locker. Even had I accepted the detective's offer of a wire, I would have been unable to bring it with me here. I was patted down carefully, and a minute later I was ushered through a series of doors that opened onto what appeared to be a large and sunny cafeteria. At the far end, on a sort of dais, stood a frowning man in a forest-green uniform, and at each of the blue tables, spaced evenly around the room, a single prisoner waited. A number of those who had waited with me on the outside already sat across from their loved ones. The old man, having left his hat behind, had a head of strong white hair. The little boy was assembling a plastic game of Battleship while his parents spoke in low tones. The rest of the men remained motionless at their tables watching the door expectantly, and as I entered, one of these stood and was Bill Cumber.

The color had come back to his face. He wore a loose gray uniform and cocked his head at me as he put out his hand.

"Hey, bro," he said. "You get all my letters?"

"I think so," I said. "I guess I wouldn't know if I didn't."

"I guess not."

"So why'd you leave me hanging? Why didn't you take my calls?"

"You grew a beard," I said.

He stroked a hand down his face. "Yeah, man, I'm all-natural. I'm off the meds, too. I'm seeing much more clearer now." He leaned forward and looked at me closely. "Let me ask you a question."

"Shoot."

"Why are you here?"

Again, I squirmed. "I'm just trying to understand what happened."

"I already told you that."

"The detectives think they can charge you with Sabine's murder. I thought—"

"That's bullcrap." He gestured toward the windows. "I'm gonna be a free man."

"I want to know about Denise."

His head turned sharply to me.

"Who told you about Denise?"

"It's in the records at the courthouse." It was true. In the run-up to this visit, I had requested copies of every document relating to William J. Cumber. There were pages and pages on Bill's one-time girlfriend, about fights, a restraining order, a final falling-out. According to the report, he had grabbed Denise's daughter by the throat one night and shouted, "Why do you defy me?" There was even a letter Denise had written some weeks later to the judge, asking that Bill not be charged with child abuse. "He just seems to be a slow learner," she wrote at the time.

Now he sat back, squinted at me, and grinned. "Man, you an investigative soul." He looked from side to side. "All right. Me and this buddy of mine had just got out—this was in North Carolina—and he says he wants to go see his lady, so we go and see her. But right off the bat, I could tell she wanted to be with me, not him. So when he went back in the other room, I asked her to roll up my sleeve."

"To roll up your sleeve?"

"Yeah, I put out my arm like this, and say, 'Could you roll up my sleeve?'" He held out his arm on the table between us. "And that was it. We was together. That was Denise."

He talked for a time about their troubles in North Carolina. He'd punched the foreman of his tree-trimming crew, and she'd maybe cashed some checks that weren't hers. So they came to Florida with her daughter.

I brought up the police report, and he looked at me again for a long time.

"I'm not proud of it," he said, "but I didn't hit her any harder than she needed to be hit." He thought again for a time. "I never judged anybody who didn't deserve to be judged."

Suddenly coming to himself again, he pulled a thick, frayed folder from his lap and set it between us. "I almost forgot something. Check this out."

He pulled from the folder a drawing of two dolphins leaping in front of a pink sunset.

"What do you think?" Bill's nose and an eye appeared to one side of the drawing. "It's two dolphins in front of a sunset."

"Nice."

"That's my art."

"You made that?"

He drew back in mock offense. "I'm an artist, man. I was starting to sell my drawings out on the island. Sabine was helping me, you know, before everything that happened happened. I had a LLC and everything. It was called Cumbervision, except with an *e* on the end, you know, so you said it like French. *Cumbervisioné.*"

He began now to pull out one page after another.

"Look at these. That's a heart. And here's one that's a honey bear. A dog with a heart-shaped nose—I call that one *The Dogtor of Love.*" A falsetto laugh shook his shoulders. He looked again at the drawing, then put it away. "Here's more dolphins."

"Bill," I said. "I want to know more about you and Sabine."

"More dolphins. I could sell a thousand of these in a minute for three dollars a piece." He nodded to himself. "I just need somebody to set up the website."

"Did you love her?"

He paused, still holding up a dolphin drawing. "Yeah, I loved her."

"What did you love?"

"She had a charm about her. You would be happy around her. Your movement changed. She cared about you. Like when I was in prison, she would send me things. Sundry items. Vitamins and shampoo, pants, shoes—she sent me a pair of Nikes once. She used to send me nail hardener."

"Nail hardener?"

"It's a hardener, you know. It doesn't sit on top of the nail. It soaks in and *hardens* it." He held up his hand and pointed at a nail. "And then when I went out to the motel on Saturdays, she would give me a manicure. She didn't like my raggedy nails. You had to look GQ for her." He pantomimed the snapping of his lapels. "Yeah, she was always working at my cuticles."

"So what happened?"

"We became destranged. We went out for dinner with her friends, and she ate in these little niblets, you know. I was afraid just to order a beer. And the language that was talked was different. These people, they looked like a skipper or a maiden, and I didn't know how to speak. She could walk around almost with her nose up in the air. I didn't want her to be around me, but in a way I did. I'm used to this," he said, and he intertwined his two index fingers. "Unity."

"Were you drinking?" I said.

His face froze for a moment. "Nah, man. I mean I'd have *a* beer, but, nah, not like that."

"Somebody I talked to said you were drinking pretty hard. They said after she disappeared, you ended up sleeping in a shed down on Fourteenth Street."

"Who said that?" He leaned toward me, searching my face, then suddenly backed away. "Nah, man, I wasn't drinking. She just thought I was going back to my old ways, hanging out with the wrong sorts of people. That's what always aggravates me about females. They knew who you was when they started dating you, then why do they want you to change?"

For a while, neither of us said anything. I thought of Erin at home in Iowa, wondered if we had become destranged, wondered what we would talk about when I returned.

"Me and you," he said. "We have some sort of repertoire."

He looked up at the clock.

"Hold up," he said. "We're about to run out of time, and I need to ask you something." He began reading the inside of his wrist. "Can you get me *A Feast for Crows*? It's book four in that Games of Thrones series."

"I'll see if I can find it. You like those?"

"Yeah, bro. I'm about to the last book."

"You know that he's still writing them?"

His forehead wrinkled. "For real?"

"Yeah, there are two more he hasn't finished. People are starting to think he doesn't know how to end it."

Bill sat silent for a moment. "Well, that's 'cause he doesn't know how to kill people."

8: All the Lives

THERE WERE A LOT of questions that I never found the answer to in Florida—sometimes because no one could tell me, often because there wasn't one. At some point during that year, for instance, it must have occurred to Tom Buehler that the course of his life had been permanently altered. Where was he when the realization came? Skimming the pool at the motel? Eating cereal and sliced grapefruit? Driving the bridge to Cortez? And what did he do? He and Sabine had long been husband and wife in name only. By that fall, he had his own girlfriend. It had been an insult that Sabine carried on her affair at the motel, and it was tempting to think Tom would have been relieved by her disappearance. In some measure, perhaps he was. However, a lover's indifference so often engenders only more love; it seemed just as likely Tom was devastated by her loss. A little while after the disappearance, beside a road on Anna Maria, a man discovered a suitcase full of photographs of Sabine. Questioned by detectives, Tom freely admitted he had put it there, and the newspapers proceeded to make some to-do over it. The event did seem important somehow, but it was difficult to say why. Eventually, everyone forgot about the abandoned suitcase. There wasn't a law against throwing things away.

I wished I could have been present during Robert Corona's brief cruise down Fourteenth. How it must have felt to swing out onto the road a few hours short of dawn, to punch the gas and roll down the windows and run the cool night air. Even a life of regular incarceration is punctuated by moments blind with the sense of possibility, and I wondered if Corona, in the quarter mile between the green light and the siren, had been allotted such a feeling of freedom.

But most of all, I was captivated by the relationship between Bill and Sabine. Had she spun her hair between two fingers when she worked? Did they ever dance? Did he know her middle name? Did he know why she was afraid of the dark? I knew that Bill had lied to me, but I knew, too, that even if he'd told me everything he remembered, it would hardly answer all the questions I had.

I had talked to one of the state's attorneys about the case. Sitting at a table stacked with papers, he'd held a pen between his hands and looked out the window. "Even when they confess," he said, "you still don't get the truth."

I left Florida that Tuesday, taking a plane from Tampa in the first hours of the morning. As a boy, the sight of the earth falling away beneath my feet had delighted me, but that day it only gave me a feeling of vague unease. I leaned my forehead against the plastic oval, as I always do, and watched the tarmac blur and disappear. The landscape flattened; the people shrank. First, the cars and the houses lost their definition, then whole neighborhoods became indistinguishable from one another. For a long time, a certain hill or highway or power plant remained apart from the mass. Soon, though, that too became another grayish fleck among many, and I was struck acutely by the sense of all the streets I would never walk, all the rooms I would never enter, all the lives not mine to live. I thought of the apartment in Iowa that no longer felt like my own, and of the woman waiting there whom I no longer knew how to love. Then with a fluttering of white, we burst through the clouds, and I closed my eyes and tried to sleep.

The arguments of lovers are such a constant that it's easy to notice only the most egregious examples—the shouted dispute in the gas station parking lot, the door slammed in the adjoining apartment, the bruised cheek, the child outside the courtroom waiting to learn who's won his custody. But it seems to me that some large part, perhaps the greater portion of this violence, since undoubtedly, even in its most mild form, it *is* violence, is carried out in low voices, or maybe without words at all, almost unconsciously, in the turning of a shoulder at the kitchen sink or the casting of a glance.

During that trip to Florida, as I traveled from the sheriff's office to the prison, as I spread the newspaper open on the passenger-side seat to review the day's fresh horrors, the fear that descended upon me was not of the cursory cruelty of human affairs but of my own part in it. When I considered the death of Sabine Musil-Buehler in its specifics—when I thought, for instance, of the blouse she chose the day she disappeared, the radio still tuned to her favorite station in the stolen car, the blood that indicated how the body, almost like a piece of luggage, had been pulled from the back seat—I recoiled in horror. I had no interest in the murder; I knew that I could never commit such a crime. But I recognized a kinship, however faint, between that act and the uncaring words that had already become a habit in my own relationship. I didn't see myself succumbing to the rage of Bill Cumber, but I knew I was capable, as my grandfather had been, of the offhand comment, the exasperated sigh, which over time can be just as lethal as physical force.

That day, as the plane reached its altitude, I felt the need to write down an account of exactly what had happened between Bill and Sabine. I could use this story as a sort of Venn diagram, it seemed to me, isolating all my own worst inclinations in the overlap and then excising them. But the story I wanted to tell could not be reconstructed from the few facts assembled by the sheriff's office. It had little to do with my note cards or my interviews. A love affair makes sense only to the lovers, and so I wanted to tell the story as Bill and Sabine might have told it, a simple story, by necessity an act of the imagination, about two people who tried, and failed, to be in love. As the Sarasota reporter had explained to me, if I wanted the truth, I would have to make it up. At that height, with the peninsula laid out below, it wasn't difficult to begin.

SEEN FROM ABOVE, Florida emerges from the continent like the appendage of an amoeba: brown and green with a border of near-white sand. The clouds sweep across it so slowly they appear not to move at all. On the Atlantic side, the ocean floor drops off steeply into a color almost black, but on the western flank, the water remains shallow and blue far out into the Gulf of Mexico.

Around the middle of the peninsula, there is a break in the line, and a two-tongued channel pushes inland forming the deepwater bay of Tampa, and here, right at the bay's mouth, is the island of Anna Maria, shaped like an elongated comma, a lump of sand and dirt in the north, trailing behind it a long drawn-out tail. Running the length of the island, almost like a spine, is a curving two-lane road, and though much of the land is taken up with houses and pools, there are also palms and banyans and oaks, and great violet shadows of bougainvillea.

The sun is beginning to rise on a few pale-yellow buildings. The breeze moves softly in the shade, carrying with it the sour reek of the canals. Having watched the whole night through, a hawk sits in a pine above the motel and dozes, and the first pelicans appear in ungainly formation on the horizon. In a rustling of nylon, two women walk past, and the first truck goes by, stirring up the sand and dust that had settled on the road in the night. The sun begins to burn on the rooftops, and one by one the air conditioners grunt and spin to life in the windows of the motel rooms. Now the people in the rooms begin to stir. A girl listens to the waves breaking. A father urinates quietly, so as not to wake his family. A woman lies in bed with the curtains drawn and tries not to think about work. For a minute, all is stillness and calm, and the guests teeter on that edge between the liquid beauty of their dreams and the solidity of life.

In the years since the motel was built, the island has been caught up in a series of construction booms and busts, each of which has left its mark. Gone are the cinder-block bungalows with corrugated roofs and screened-in porches, and with them, the retired fighter pilots standing watch over a barbecue while their wives mix pitchers of concentrate. In their place have arisen a progression of vacation homes: the 1980s deco, with its tube-steel railings and glass brick windows; and next door, the terra-cotta Tuscan villa with a smoked-glass cupola and automatic hurricane shutters. The newest houses sport a lighthearted Gothic style: aluminum roofs and pastel siding, and white finials that taper into fine, pike points. Now, in early 2008, with the latest construction frenzy nearing its peak, the road by the motel is jammed, even though the sun has been up only an hour, with cement mixers and pile drivers and flatbeds loaded with thirty-foot palms, the rental cars of tourists, and the contractors' sparkling new pickups. From this stream of pickup trucks, one diverges, cuts across the road, and pulls into a space outside the motel.

Through the blinds on the glass door, the sun throws a series of slanted stripes across the objects in the motel office, revealing on its surface a room almost indistinguishable from a thousand other motel offices. There is a desk full of papers, a calendar with an image of footprints on a beach, a varnished plywood board with rows of brass keys hanging from nails. On one wall, a black plastic credit-card machine is mounted, and on the desk there is a large gray computer. In a corner, a rack lists to the side beneath the weight of brochures: Captain Kathe's boat trips, Fish Hole miniature golf. In a cage by the office door, the only sign of eccentricity: a green parrot, its head tucked beneath its wing.

This parrot is too apt. I recall that Poe, in his first conception of the raven, envisioned a parrot, and it is so patently a literary device that I would reject the idea out of hand if I hadn't once seen him. He is dappled green, the same dappled green of the forests that were his homeland. His eyelids are chalky and gray. In the final minutes of sleep, they twitch restlessly. How old he is, what images hurtle through his brain in that avian dark, we can't say with certainty any more than he could. But if he is a bird, he must sing. When Tom Buehler steps down from his pickup truck, the parrot wakes with a start and launches into the monologue that will carry him through evening: nursery rhymes and snippets of conversation, and thanks to a persistent nine-year-old from Queens who stayed here last summer, the occasional murmur of "Asshole, asshole, asshole."

No great leap of the imagination is required to fathom the feelings of a man for his wife's parrot, especially if the marriage has soured. He doesn't give the bird a glance. "Asshole back at you," he says, and passes by. Tom wears a faded polo, white shorts, and tennis sneakers, and after a hunt for his keys—they were in his pocket all along—he unlocks the office door. The room remains cool and dim from the night, and for a few minutes, in that pleasant half dark, he sits with his eyes closed, not yet prepared to think about anything.

It seems that both too much time and not enough has passed when the mailman knocks at the office door. He cups a hand to the glass, smiling as he peers in. From his bag, he pulls a few handfuls of catalogues and envelopes, and plods off to the next delivery. There are announcements of patio furniture sales and one-time offers at new low interest rates; solicitations for abandoned dogs, for hungry children, for rivers and trees. Among these is a letter in a plain white envelope. Addressed to Tom in rounded, almost girlish script, it has no return mark. On the back, a faint blue stamp bears the imprint *State of Florida, Department of Corrections*.

Tom doesn't open it. These letters have been coming every two weeks for the past year. They're from a man he once hired to do odd jobs around the motel. Three days he worked with Tom, and on the third, the deputies arrived. With all the guests watching, the man was arrested for arson. The letters all say the same thing: *I need help. I need a friend. I need money.* Tom is a kind person, but he's also a businessman. Who knows how his clientele was affected when the cruiser pulled into the lot. Without even bothering to crumple it, he drops the letter in the trash.

Most of the guests have already gone off on their adventures by the time Sabine arrives that afternoon in her convertible. She is a woman who prefers her mornings to herself, and at this hour, her hair is still damp from the shower. In her left hand, she carries a mug, of coffee or maybe of tea, which she tries to keep from spilling as with the right hand she maneuvers a cardboard box from the passenger seat. If she doesn't radiate happiness and contentment, she at least seems to have about her an openness to the day's sensations. She bumps the car door closed with her hip and grimaces at the swirling dust kicked up by the traffic. The bird shrieks her name as she enters the office, as she lowers the box to the floor, as she raises the mug to her lips, and he does not stop shrieking until she has gone over to the cage and said a few words to him and filled his dishes with seed and water. Tom is nowhere to be seen, but the letter is still there in the wastebasket.

She opens it, and her eyes follow the words, but she is not really reading. She is thinking the toilet in room 12 is still leaking, the cable bill is past due, she's supposed to meet Ellen for lunch. When she gets to the end of the letter, she returns it to the trash; it has done little to stir her compassion. By the time she reaches the storage room and unpacks the box of toilet paper, she has forgotten everything but the man's name: William J. Cumber. But as the day goes on, the letter resurfaces in her mind from time to time. Something in it, the care with which it was written, the abjectness of it, or perhaps something in how casually she had dismissed it, keeps her from forgetting it entirely. At the end of the day, she is working at the computer when suddenly she stops and pulls the letter out of the trash again. She reads it more slowly this time, and when she is done, she gets a page of letterhead and writes the man a kind but firm explanation of why the motel will be unable to help him. *Dear Mr. Cumber* . . .

She sends this letter Tuesday morning. On Friday, the mailman leaves a plain white envelope addressed to Sabine Musil-Buehler.

9:   Furlough

BILL KNOWS IT'S MORNING when the man two cells down begins to clear his throat. Soon, the steel door at the end of the hall clanks open, the guard's sneakers squelch along the linoleum corridor, and one of the other inmates, an Arkansas boy, begins whistling "Yankee Doodle."

The window in Bill's cell is three feet high and about the width of a spread palm, and slowly, as if thinking to itself, the sky within that rectangle swirls and brightens. The window looks out on the exercise yard and beyond it to another cellblock, and by sitting up in bed and pressing his face all the way to one side, Bill can see a tree out on the boulevard beyond the prison fence. More often, with the bedsheet wrapped around him, he looks up at the sky, a prism of blue across which planes pass silently a few times an hour. Puddle jumpers to Sarasota, someone told him, but that's just hearsay. They could be going anywhere.

The halls resound with the shouts and mutters of men as they file in a line, one by one, toward the cafeteria. With half a cigarette tucked behind his ear, Bill follows along. At his table, he moves the food around his plate, listening as this or that man reads aloud from a letter. He has taken the cigarette down from his ear and is turning it in his fingers when someone slaps him on the shoulder and says he has mail.

The letter has already been opened by the guards, and when he holds it up, the ragged edge of the slit envelope is illuminated by the fluorescent ceiling light. Most of the prisoners have finished their meals, and the room is loud with talk and the clatter of plates and cups. Even though he's sitting down, he can't get his eyes to focus on the small, neat handwriting. The words are jumbled on the paper. He finally pushes his tray away and smooths the letter out over the tabletop, then moves his fingers along beneath the lines as he reads.

"Who wrote you?" his cellmate says.

"Your sister."

"Shut up."

When he finishes, his eyes return to one phrase. *I wish there were more I could do.*

His cellmate pulls the envelope across the table and inspects the handwriting. "A lady."

FROM THE PRISON in St. Petersburg to the motel is about an hour and a half, and from that day forward hardly a week goes by that the mail truck doesn't carry one of his letters with it over the bridge and across Tampa Bay.

When her second letter arrives, he rushes through it once. When he comes to some noteworthy moment, a particularly kind word, a revelation of some aspect of her personality, he calls out to his cellmate and reads the passage aloud. Having arrived at the end, he scrutinizes the signature—looking for what, he couldn't say—and satisfying himself with its authenticity, he returns to the beginning and rushes through the letter again. He reads it more times than he can remember, each time gleaning a little more meaning, and each time causing his cellmate to stare out the window with a little more studious disinterest.

The other inmates glory over the carnal hints in their own letters, but the things that delight Bill aren't anything scandalous, just a strange turn of phrase or a word he doesn't know and will have to look up. He likes the foreignness of her letters. She knows words he doesn't, but he knows how to use them. When he's read it through the final time, it is no longer the letter it was at the beginning. It has become something else entirely, a part of him almost, and he could point out with complete certainty—in his mind, he does point out—exactly where this or that word was on the page. With her phrases cluttering his thoughts, he smells the letter and folds it and puts it beneath his mattress and closes his eyes. But a moment later, he has drawn it out and is reading once more. He holds it up close to his eyes and sees the way she's written his name.

When Sabine finds one of Bill's letters on the desk, she leaves it there, and at the end of the day, she puts it in her purse. She has nothing to hide, after all; she just wishes someone would realize it. She goes to the bank and the grocery store, the beach and the city council meeting, and all that time, the letter is waiting. She sees it sometimes, getting out her checkbook or the key to her car, and already there is the sense that she is bound on a sort of path. The letter could stay there at the bottom of her purse for days. More than once, she waits so long that another letter arrives before she's opened the one previous. But finally, some morning when she knows she'll have a few minutes to herself, she sits down at home with a cup of tea and reads.

If her first letters are short and polite, his are long and full of questions. Written on state-issued paper, they feel greasy, like newsprint, on her fingers. Despite her calm, her thrill is the greater of the two, and though she doesn't rush headlong through the reading, this is only because she pauses purposely between sentences to slow herself down. She enjoys his attention, the way his thoughts seem to run out onto the page unmediated, and she doesn't want the pleasure of reading to drain away too quickly. When she finishes, she immediately writes a reply, addresses it, and affixes a stamp, and only then does she realize she's forgotten to drink her tea.

She mails the letter and drives home to have dinner with Tom, and it's as if the knowledge that Bill is waiting for her reply has buffered her against the frustrations of everyday life. Rain, a flat tire, the lewd suggestions of an old man who stops to help her with the jack: What do these amount to in the face of another human being's care? Tom cares about her, of course, but it's not the same.

For Bill's part, the task of replying is always fraught. Days he carries one of her letters around with him everywhere he goes. He has become bashful about it and no longer shows it off. He has finally succeeded in leaving the letter behind, going down for a few minutes to the exercise yard or for his shift in the mess, but five minutes haven't passed when he begins to wonder if it really was as sincere as he first believed. When his shift is done, he rushes back to his cell and pulls the stack of letters out from beneath the mattress. He reads the most recent one painstakingly now, word by word, and notices how certain passages have been oddly phrased, and he frets until lights-out. And for a long while after the room goes dark, he still is weighing how much she meant the things she said.

In the morning, returned by a night of sleep to cautious confidence, he writes a careful reply, throws it away, then dashes off another and sends it without reading it.

There is something holy in a friendship born like this in letters. The meditative mind-set so often absent from writing and from bodily love is heaped upon the letter. The mind traces every word as though it were the line of a cheek. There is the sense of being extrapolated from oneself, of sending one's message by carrier pigeon across vast, dark, and lonely landscapes. We drift pleasantly into hyperbole and, describing the dull act of waking up, we are carried away into a lexicon made giddy with precision. It hardly matters what these letters say. Sabine might write about the rain, the dreary rain, as she lies alone in one of the motel rooms. Bill might write about that morning's breakfast, or a dream he had, or a pair of inmates, both named Frankie. It doesn't matter; that giddiness is all they hope to communicate.

To her, he is earnest and enthusiastic. He could write for pages about his plans for the future and the obstacles he would easily overcome. As much as she smiles at his boyishness, his foolhardiness, she also finds it impossible not to be caught up in his galloping excitement. He is going to live by selling his art, by becoming a carpenter. He has read a book about cowboys and is heading west to rustle steer. The moment she puts the letter away with the others and goes out with a glass of wine to sit by the canal, she sees quite clearly the ridiculousness of his plans. She knows he is no cowboy, but still she sees him in a wide-brimmed hat.

They fill their letters with questions. She asks him about the food in prison. He asks her about sea turtles. She asks whether his cellmate ever reads their letters. He asks if she would send him another twenty-five dollars. She asks how he will get out West. He asks what Germany was like. And these questions continue back and forth until finally he asks again if she'll let him work at the motel on Saturdays. She will have to talk to Tom, she writes, and he probably won't like the idea. In fact, she knows Tom will hate the idea of her bringing Bill Cumber to the motel, just as she knows she will do it anyway.

She is surprised by the prison—a small building with a red roof—and by how easy it is to enter. She shows the guard her identification, and soon she's in a windowless room, sitting with her legs crossed in a cold plastic chair. She doesn't know what she'd expected, but not this. When he is led into the waiting room, she stands and smiles a little too purposefully, and seeing this, he can think of nothing to say except to remark what a beautiful morning it is.

It is a beautiful morning. The sun is still low when they walk outside, and the heat is only beginning to paw at the edges of the day. Herds of clouds range across the blue sky with dignity and purpose, and as the two of them leave the prison behind, he is overwhelmed by the simple facts of the morning: a child running across a lawn with a doll and a spatula; the smell of bacon and bilge water; a pile of oranges in the shade on the roadside; a man at a deserted street corner, proclaiming the end of the world on a rumpled square of cardboard.

She is older than he'd remembered. It hasn't been so long—a year maybe—since he worked at the motel. He'd seen her a few times before the deputies arrived. He thought she had long blond hair, but now it's cut to her shoulders and silver. Her hands are small and white, with short-clipped nails and smooth, thin scars along the fingers. From what? He pretends to look at a tanker out on the bay and examines her profile, silhouetted against the green blur of leaves outside her window. Her forehead is high; her nose, blunt. In her sunglasses, the road mercators out broadly, and behind them, her eyes, hidden in a pocket of shadow, look soft. He leans back and rests, and like the child who has fallen asleep on the drive home, he wants nothing more than for this ride to go on forever. When the car slows, and shells crunch beneath the tires, it takes him a few moments to remember he is looking at the motel.

None of the guests are up yet, but Tom is sitting in the office, and the two men shake hands stiffly. Sabine leads Bill from one place to the next. Here are the cleaning supplies; here, the tools for sweeping, trimming, weeding. She ticks off a list of work to be done, and like that, she's gone, and he is holding a broom.

Amid the palms and pastel walls and the slapping water of the pool and the cries of aggrieved seagulls, he works as if consumed by a whole and private joy, a joy not simply in his speech, but in his arms and legs, as well. If he is hammering a part of the deck back into place, it's certain that he'll hammer a few other things—a loose piece of siding, a lounge chair—out of sheer magnanimity. He waters the plants as though offering a blessing, and when he's cleaned the windows in a room, he spends a few minutes just staring out at the pool.

At lunch, he takes a turkey sandwich down to the beach and eats it with his feet in the surf. When a heron stalks up next to him, he says, "No way, buddy." Two minutes later, he's throwing her crusts. When there's no sandwich left, he holds up his hands to show that it's gone, but she knows better than to believe him. "Shoo," he says, and she flaps her wings a little, not really flying, just making a show, and settles soundlessly out of arm's reach.

In the afternoon, a black-haired girl comes to sit behind the desk and hand customers their keys. And a woman appears in the hut by the pool to launder the sheets and towels from the night before. He doesn't say anything to them, and they don't say anything to him. Sabine is nowhere to be seen, but he keeps working as if she were standing over him with a stopwatch. His back aches; his knees are sore. Cleaning hair from the pool's filter, he can't wait for the work to be done, and he doesn't even notice when she walks up beside him.

"Time's up," she says, and he turns to find her smiling down at him with her purse over her shoulder. She goes and stands beside the car while he soaps his hands in the slop sink. He feels the irritable pride of work only begun, and holding his hands beneath the steaming water, he rinses them until they're raw and red, and then pokes his head in the office to say goodbye to Tom.

"It was OK?" Sabine says as he gets in the car.

"I like the work."

There is a lightness to him when he returns to prison that day. "Next week?" he says, and when she nods, he saunters back into his cellblock.

"You win the lottery?" says one of the guards.

A FEW WEEKENDS at the motel are enough for Bill to understand the range of the clientele: a couple on their anniversary, a pair of suburban teens down from Indiana with fake New Jersey IDs, four stylish men from Scandinavia, an antiquarian bookseller, his glasses greased with fingerprints, waiting for a convention in Sarasota. By and large, the guests are there for only a night or a week, but out of their sex and disputations and lost room keys, a culture does flow. Bill only has to pause outside the guests' windows to hear a man complaining to his wife about the hair in the sink; an Italian woman crying out just short of satisfaction; the hissing of two children over a plastic shovel; the scrape of pages turning in a book.

When guests arrive, he leaves off what he's doing, and heads to the office. The girl tells him the room number, and he picks up their bags.

Tess is the girl's name. She's skinny, with an open hopeful face, and her aspirations aren't a secret. Her mother likes nothing more than to talk to Tom and Sabine about how Tess wants to be in film, as though by saying it aloud she can make it untrue. Tess looks on her mother with pity, as she looks on most adults, whose lives—now that she's begun to pay attention—seem mainly composed of doctor appointments, vegetables, and concerns about money. She is determined not to become like the sad couples who check into the motel with new suitcases and a sulking child, and each morning, before she leaves for work, she takes a Flintstones vitamin and a birth control pill. She isn't haughty, as her mother said a few years ago; she simply refuses to be unhappy. She works as diligently as a person can who is waiting for her life to begin. She says little, does less, and passes the unbearable afternoons with crosswords, number games, anything to make it go a little more quickly.

From this monotony, only Sabine offers some relief. Sabine doesn't smile on her dismissively when she talks about her plans after high school. Sabine isn't beholden to anyone. She does what she wants. And she once dated a movie star, though he was a German movie star. Tess has a passionate interest in movie stars, particularly in the deaths of starlets. If by twenty-seven she has not landed a role in a major motion picture, even only as a supporting actress, she plans to commit suicide, though even suicide, she has to admit, seems less fulfilling when one is not yet famous.

She doesn't even notice the man who's started doing odd jobs around on Saturdays until Sabine tells her she's brought a felon to work at the motel.

"Am I crazy?" Sabine says.

"What did he do wrong?" says Tess.

"A few things," Sabine says.

Bill Cumber seems harmless to her. As far as she can tell, he's perfectly content to sweep around the pool. In his blue jeans and tight white undershirts, he reminds her a little of pictures of James Dean from *Rebel Without a Cause*, which she should see.

"Well, if you haven't seen that," Bill says to her, "then have you seen *One Flew Over the Cuckoo's Nest*?"

"Is that James Dean, too?"

"I don't know what to say. You need to understand the quality of confinement . . ." Bill walks off with the suitcases, still talking to himself.

Just as Tess's dreams are of a life beyond Anna Maria, Britta's dreams have led her to the island and to the little hut where she sits folding the laundry. She's German, like Sabine, and she's part of the shifting cast of expatriates at the motel. Two years ago she separated from her husband and came to Florida to forget him. She has not made much headway, but even trying feels like progress. Every morning, when the sun brightens her curtains, Britta wakes up in Germany. She hears the bus going around the traffic circle and sees outside her window, beyond the row of houses, a field of sunflowers, a low stone wall and a forest of spruces. It isn't until the AC unit kicks on outside that the row houses fold up, the *Wald* flattens, and her husband's car vanishes. She rolls over and looks out the window and between two large vacation homes, she can just make out a glittering patch of the Gulf.

Britta has not made many friends on Anna Maria, but of the few, Sabine is the one who's been most kind. Sabine found her an apartment, and it was Sabine, too, who hired her at the motel so she could stay in the country. She also took her to get her hair cut, dragged her along to parties, invited her on cruises, and one day showed up with two plastic tubs of scrapbooking supplies and a bottle of prosecco. Britta's reward is that Sabine tells her everything and listens to everything she has to say. It is to Britta that Sabine confides the lack of love she feels for Tom, and it is from Sabine's silence on the subject of Bill that Britta knows there is more than she is saying.

Britta recognizes an insidious aspect of their friendship, as well. The pale-blue curtains through which the sun breaks each morning, these were picked out at Sabine's insistence. The unused orange-juicer on the counter, it's an exact replica of the one Sabine and Tom have at home. And the embroidered Mexican dress she wears as she sits by the pool, it was Sabine who told her she looked beautiful in it. It is not lost on Britta that, like the seagull with the broken wing or the cardboard box of kittens, she would be much less interesting to Sabine if she didn't require mending.

"Feel this." Bill hands her a wrench he's found in the workroom. "That sucker's heavy, isn't it? Now *that's* a tool." And he walks off, looking for things to tighten.

He works hard, Britta can see, but he doesn't have the faculties to occupy himself beyond his work. Any time there is a pause—when he must wait for a box of screws or a new battery—he smokes one cigarette after another, or goes out and disappears on the beach. Or he throws himself down into the chair beside her and launches into a story about a crocodile or the food at prison or a boy he once knew who was born with six fingers and six toes, pointing out the place on his hand where the scar was, and as he speaks, he twists a dirty rag into knots, or shreds a palm leaf until at last, having worked up a little havoc in himself, he springs from the chair and, still talking, goes out front to smoke another cigarette. He's lost his train of thought by the time he returns, and now he wants to know what Sabine thinks of him, does she ever talk about him, what does she say?

ONLY ONE BUILDING on the property is two stories. The second floor, reached by a set of wooden outdoor stairs, contains a large room with pink travertine tile, a California king bed up against one wall, and a bathtub with Jacuzzi jets. Sabine calls it the honeymoon suite. On the ground floor, beneath the suite, is a store-room and workshop. On hot days, the air in this first-floor room is so thick you can hardly breathe, but when the weather's cool, Bill doesn't mind hiding there awhile and resting his eyes. There's a workbench covered in lug-wrench heads, bottles of dried-up wood glue, a rusted saw. A mattress with a terrific stain leans against one wall, and in front of it, a group of broken chairs sit in a circle as though to console themselves in one another's company.

Sabine has asked him to repair a number of the treads on the stairs to the suite, and he approaches the task with ceremony. The metallic snap of the measuring tape, and the bump of the pencil over the wood's rough grain; the feeling of a piece of lumber in his hands, and the shuddering as the saw bites into the wood; the rhythm of the saw, its purposeful sliding back and forth, and how the board, which he has pinned beneath one knee, tries to wrest itself from under his weight; the sawdust dropping into a pile on the cement floor, and the lighter dust drifting up into the bev-eled sunshine; the furred edges of the wood along the cut, and the damp warmth that rises on his back: all these things carry a nearly religious weight for him, and when he touches the blade with his hand, he is surprised to remember that it's hot.

In this way, the stairs come slowly, piece by piece, a project scattered over a number of weeks. When he cuts one of the planks too short, he tells Sabine he will need to get more wood, and she is cross. She scolds him for his carelessness—it has not been the first time—and stands beside the stairs while he goes back to work. He loves this displeasure of hers, the half-stern look on her face as he sets to sanding, and so does she, he thinks. Already, she is incapable of being truly unhappy with him. They play their parts well, and when he sings "Sixteen Tons," sawing with long dramatic strokes, he catches her smiling.

He's beneath the stairs putting in some screws when Sabine goes to clean the room on the second floor, and without thinking, he glances up as she passes overhead. Flickering in the open spaces between the treads, he sees her two legs stretching up above him, soft and white from the calves to the tightened tendons in her knees and continuing on for the briefest of moments to a terminus that he feels obliged to turn away from. On occasions such as this, he finds Britta in the laundry hut and narrates for her such portions of his feelings as make her cross herself.

"Hopeless," she says, pulling a towel from his hands.

"Britta." He pats her on the knee. "Don't pretend you haven't done it."

"Go." She pushes him out of the seat and sets to refolding the towel he has rumpled.

Toward the end of the day, it seems like he's alone at the motel. Sabine has disappeared into one of the rooms with a package of lightbulbs. Tom is nowhere to be seen, and Britta has finished her laundry. All the guests have jet-skied off to the deserted fort on the next island over, or they've headed up to watch the manatees rolling around in the hot-water runoff at the power plant. It's just he and Tess, who is delicately picking her nose in the office. As the hour draws near when he must return to his cell, he imagines what the motel must look like at dawn or dusk, by the pool with a can of beer, and the clouds blocking out the stars. The blueness of evening, how all that is white is swayed to blue, the sand, the stucco, the sidewalk and mortar, the sun-bleached phone poles, and the sheets hung out to dry by the widow next door. How the sea turns from gold to silver, and the eye of the heron dilates hungrily. How the road goes quiet, and the deputy in the church lot puts the car in park and rests his eyes. The great freshness in the air at night as a rainstorm approaches, the concentration of smells, of gasoline and oleander. All that he has seen, all that he has done, is dissolved into the thought of that which remains beyond his reach, as if the things he imagines are more durable, more real, than those that stand before him.

10: Ballad of the Estranged Husband

TOM HAS LIVED IN Florida a few decades, meaning he is as close as most people get to being a local. He would know then, I suppose, the quickest way from one place to another and where not to get your hair cut, and he probably remembers what the bridge to Longboat Key looked like before they put in the new concrete pilings. Whenever a recent transplant complains about the tourists, Tom is careful not to take sides. He remembers what it was like when he first came to Anna Maria, how empty the beach feels sometimes. "Nobody has it easy," his father used to say, and when a woman cuts him off in traffic, he tries to imagine what life looks like from her point of view, just as I am trying to imagine what life looks like from his. He is one of the rare locals who doesn't in the least resent the tourist and the newcomer, perhaps because he tries to make his living off them.

He has a compact build, and when he stands still, he stands with his feet set a little wide. But he does not stand still often, and he is usually rushing from the office to the laundry machine or from the beach to the bank. When he speaks, his hands move swiftly before him, as if unsure where to settle. His face is handsome but coarse—thick lips, a snub nose—and he is always rubbing a hand across his mouth or over his eyes, as though beneath them were a finer set of features. He walks quickly, as well, and his thoughts come on with such rapidity that he can never bring the words out fast enough.

Had he been able to focus his tremendous energy on one task at a time, he might have accomplished feats to awe the world, but instead it seems it is the energy itself that, through sheer quantity and force, has undermined many of his endeavors even as they were beginning. When he arrives at the bank, he is sure to have forgotten the deposit slip at home, and returning for the second time to the same teller, a patient young woman, he has now misplaced the checks he'd meant to deposit. Much of each day he spends like this, moving from place to place, beginning a thousand projects. "Slow down," Sabine tells him. "You need to slow down." But he's already thinking about what he needs to do next. For some time, his hammer has been sitting on the roof of the motel.

Like many businessmen, he has sued and been sued, has satisfied and not satisfied his mortgages, has declared bankruptcy, and has signed those innumerable pieces of paper, deeds, bank documents, and certificates of satisfaction that compose a life. With so much paperwork, he must have a lawyer, in an office maybe on Manatee Avenue in Bradenton, a few rooms in what had once been a carriage house. The parking lot needs to be repainted, and this lawyer, a long-suffering man who bears his clients' deficiencies as though they were his own, rubs his nose as Tom enters the room. Tom has ushered three marriages into this office, and the belongings he has thus far forfeited amount to more than either of them can bear to itemize, let alone total, though the lawyer keeps an informal tally. "A Buddhist, no?" he says, looking over his glasses. "Worldly things mean nothing to you?"

Tom is not confounded by most women. Though he had not been lucky in his previous marriages, he could see the reasons why. But he is confounded by Sabine. With Sabine, no sooner had they met than they were married, and no sooner were they married than their love began to cool. One day, she simply divided the house in two and asked that he stay on his side. What confuses him is that she still cares for him. She still makes him dinner every night; he makes her breakfast each morning. They've slept in separate bedrooms for years, and he has recently begun to date, but still he feels when he comes home and finds her dozing on the couch with the news on, when she wakes and looks up at him with half-closed eyes, still he feels she looks on him as her husband.

Tom remembers the day Bill Cumber was arrested at the motel, and he remembers the day the man returned alongside Sabine in the convertible. He was an enthusiastic man who responded to most questions with a nod and a smile. Now whenever there is a project that requires both men—a room needs to be repainted, a new air conditioner has to be installed—Tom tries his best to be pleasant and civil, and Bill is always more than happy to help. But Tom does sometimes watch carefully from the shade, running his hands over his sun-browned scalp, as the younger man seats himself in a patch of sunlight by the pool and shakes the sawdust from his hair.

The lover who suspects his beloved of being unfaithful is always making a case for a thing he is unable to believe is true, and so at the same time as Tom accumulates his suspicions, he denies what it is that they amount to. While he worries over the tone of Sabine's voice or the hours she spends away from the motel, he also manages somehow not to register the rumors that cross his path. He hears from Chuck Greevy that a man named Bill was out on the beach with Sabine, or Tess mentions that they went out for lunch together. He notices one day that Bill is not working at all but lying by the pool with cotton balls between his toes. He doesn't say anything or ask any questions. It's hard enough to stay focused without pursuing these avenues of thought. He puts the whole thing out of his mind, and begins looking for his tape measure.

AT NOON, BILL has to call and check in with his corrections officer. He does this from the old white landline in the office, flipping through the *Far Side* calendar while Tom, on the other side of the desk, swings side to side in the swivel chair.

"Cumber," he says. "William. Number oh-two-nine-one-two."

There is no hold music. The thunder out on the Gulf sounds like cargo shifting in the belly of a big ship. While Bill waits, Tom watches as the shadows outside fade and disappear and the cars begin to go by with their headlights on. The palms shake their heads, and with the first raindrops, Tess shows up holding a bag of takeout with a boy from high school behind her, the rain beading on his spiked hair. Only when the rain is falling in straight lines and frothing on the road does Sabine appear, plunging into the room in a soaked pair of overalls. It is not a large office. On the one side of the desk, Tom and Tess and the boyfriend are packed together. Bill and Sabine are on the other side.

In some way, despite his efforts, the possibility has crept into Tom's mind that something untoward has begun to occur. When the storm passes, and everyone else leaves the office, he remains standing by the open door, and without even realizing, he begins to consider offhandedly how much he despises Bill.

11: Explicable Phenomena

WE TREAT THE TIDES as commonplace. We send monkeys into space as simply as if we were sending flowers to our mother. We fertilize our strawberries with the bones of ancient sharks and light our bathrooms by perturbing an isotope of uranium. We carry on unwondering in a world of explicable phenomena, and in this state of mind, how do we approach the subject of love?

Sabine ignores it. She has plenty to do and to think about, and the man she picks up on Saturday mornings and drops off on Saturday evenings is only one part of the day's many obligations. She fills up the convertible with unleaded, reads her horoscope between bites of cereal, buys and returns a redder shade of lipstick, and generally goes about her life as though nothing has changed. She and Bill continue to exchange letters, and she writes out her replies in the same careful, considerate hand that she uses for all her other business. When he disappears back into the prison, she makes a point of not dallying in the parking lot. She is a woman with six credit cards, and she has things to do.

It's on her ride home, however, that she finds herself subject to a not-yet-conscious heightening of the senses. It is spring, the time of year in that part of Florida when for weeks on end the air is precisely the temperature of the skin, and as she drives back to Anna Maria a little before dusk, the streetlamps pop on, and the world feels to her like the set of a movie where all your neighbors like you and want you to do well. She can't help noticing things that before she'd never given her attention—the boys using oranges for baseballs in an empty corner lot, the woman leaning against the bathroom door at the gas station, the ads for swimming lessons on the bus benches—and by the time she returns home from dropping him off, she already has three things she'd like to put in her next letter. She thinks that she should write them down before she forgets, and sitting in the driveway with the dash light on, she turns to one of the blank pages at the back of her checkbook and discovers that it's already full of notes.

FOR A LONG time she has been meaning to get back in shape, and on a Wednesday afternoon, her day off from work, she drives to Sarasota to meet with a personal trainer named Armando. He speaks with a faint Cuban lisp, his cheeks are dark, despite the closeness of his shave, and his sleeveless shirt hangs like a curtain from the muscles on his chest.

"How many times a week, baby?"

"What do you think?"

"Let's see your tummy." He looks over his clipboard as she hesitates. "Oh, honey, you're a woman. Have some pride."

He looks her over quickly. "Three times a week."

She takes out her checkbook.

"Cash only, but don't you worry. Get me next time." He smiles. "I never asked you: What's his name?"

"Who?"

So Sabine Musil-Buehler finds herself on the trajectory of love and discovers that the path is well-worn. On Saturday mornings at the prison, she's one of many women there to sign out a man for furlough. There is a group of older women who seem to have known one another for years. They sit in the waiting room together, arguing in English and Spanish—about glucosamine tablets, the warden, the governor, their children, who are raising their grandchildren the wrong way—and when a name is called, they gather their things and nod to the rest of the group. Here and there, a few young women sit with their legs crossed, pulling down their skirts every so often. The rest, like Sabine, are somewhere in between. They look blurred, as though there were a gap between what they thought their lives would be and what they have become, and the discrepancy has kept them from fully solidifying. A few bring children; most step outside to have a cigarette while they wait. Sabine cannot find much to sympathize with in these women, who all seem to her to suffer from some deep deficiency, and when Bill appears in the doorway, she is already on her feet.

Her stomach is so sore from her workout that she can hardly turn to look at him in the car. She feels like there's an iron rod running up the middle of her spine, and she can't raise her arms above the level of her shoulders. But this aching feels akin to elation.

It is still early, and the sky is flakked with high, translucent clouds. The roads are empty, and the sound of the engine dissipates across the wide lawns. They drive for a long while beneath that sky, listening to nothing but the wind in their ears, and just as morning seems to have returned the world to a past age, so Sabine also feels the presence of Bill has allowed her to return to some earlier and more expectant time of her life. In her fourteen years in Florida, she has grown skilled at seeing only the things she's seen a thousand times before: the spinning racks of sunglasses and the taillights of the cars in front of her. But the world on these mornings seems to have been composed of a different substance than the rest. She is aware of the dazzle of shattered glass on the side of the road, the white needlelike masts of sailboats rocking in their slips, the gentle banking of the highway that shifts her slightly in her seat, inclining her body toward his. Everything has been charged with the possibility of being noticed, and she feels the world has been favored with a forgotten lightness. When they crest the apex of the bridge, her stomach rises slightly.

"You know," he says, "the second I saw this car . . ."

"What?"

"I said, 'She's all right.'"

"'All right' is good?"

"I mean it's pretty cool for a lady like you to have a car like this."

"A lady like me?"

He scooches around in his seat.

"I guess I thought you'd be a little stuck on yourself, hoity-toity. I never hung out with a woman of quality, you know."

"Hung out."

"Yeah," he says. "Hanging out."

"How did you hang out"—she changes lanes—"with other women?"

"Well, it's a fluid concept."

She looks over at him, and he smiles and looks out the window.

"Hey," he says. "You ever see how fast this thing can go?"

They stop for breakfast at a strip-mall diner east of Bradenton. It sits in a narrow space between a gym and a nail salon, and above the plate-glass windows, a sign shows a cartoon of an old man flipping pancakes. Inside, the air is cool and smells of burned potatoes and nail-polish remover. The hostess wears a purple bow in her hair and waves two menus at them as she walks off toward a booth along the back wall. They pass a white-haired man staring out a window with a grape skewered on the end of his fork. Through a long opening in the wall, Sabine sees the chef at the kitchen sink testing his blood sugar.

The waitress arrives with two empty mugs and two carafes.

"Decaf or regular?"

The coffee smells like the vinyl on the seats and tastes like cigarettes.

Bill's appetite is stunning: three eggs, home fries, sausage, bacon, toast, an omelet, an order of pancakes, two glasses of juice. His elbows out to his sides, he eats rapidly but without method, seeming to fork food at random from the jumble on his plate. He drinks the coffee like it's water. The tabletop is littered with empty cream containers.

"So what do you want to do when you get out?"

"I've got some friends in North Carolina still," he says. "Depends on where I can get work."

"Would you miss it here?"

"Not the cops."

"Well." She finds a napkin and brushes it across her lips. "You're always welcome to put me as a reference. Tom or me."

"I can tell you one thing," he says. "I'm sure not going back to prison—I'll tell you that much."

He runs the last bites of his pancake through the yolk on his plate.

"I have an idea," she says finally. "I think you should marry Britta."

He stops chewing and looks up at her. "She needs to stay in the country," Sabine says. "There's nothing wrong with it. People do it all the time."

"I can't marry Britta," he says. "She's not my type."

"Your type. What does that matter? She's nice." Sabine crosses her arms. "What is your type?"

"I don't know," he says. "Someone like you."

When he excuses himself to go to the bathroom, the sounds swell to life in a clattering of crockery and voices. At the table beside her, a group of elderly women are having a conversation as though it were an argument.

"If Deborah says it's Waterford, it's Waterford."

"This food is too salty."

"Well, if everything's too salty, why are you eating it?"

"I just said everything's salty, and who says Deborah is the expert."

ALL THAT DAY, without meaning to, she puts herself in his way, and by that miracle of small intent, they run into each other continually. The plumber is coming, and this is enough reason for her to wait around, and to invite Bill to take a break with her. It would be silly not to on such a nice day. She decides to finally replace the leaking air conditioner in room 9, and in the parking lot of the hardware store, she follows Bill as he carries the enormous box to her car. Afterward, she is so embarrassed by the transparency of her affection that she avoids him the rest of the day. The trip back to the prison they spend in strained, amiable silence, driving with the top down so there's no obligation to speak.

The moment she drops Bill off, it's as though the world snaps back into focus. The dusk glows more pinkly, the B-minor chord strikes more deeply, the cold is more bracing, and the melon tastes more like melon. She wonders if he is lying on the cot in his cell or holding out a hand in the exercise yard to see if it's raining. Is there still a stain on his shirt where she tried to clean off the maple syrup? Is he laughing at something someone said? These intervals of separation are the most crucial moments, when the figure sprouts in the mind, grows its loveliness like leaves.

WITHOUT REALIZING IT, they have been waiting, not for a moment alone, but for a party, a crowded room—any situation where at last they can achieve some connection across the tumult of bodies and suggest escape. It is Britta's birthday. There are streamers and hats. It has all been Sabine's doing. She throws the party at lunch beside the motel pool so Bill can attend. She isn't sure who else will come, but it turns out she need not have worried. Everyone shows up right on time. Britta sits in her usual seat in the laundry hut, a few of the motel's guests round out the occasion, and it feels strangely comfortable.

"K-O-S-C-I-U-S-Z-K-O," the bookseller from room 9 says. "It's Polish, spelled like the hero of the Revolutionary War."

"Oh," says a woman. "I don't know anything about Polish history."

An old man with a liver-spotted forehead pats the bookseller on the knee. "I think it's an excellent name."

Slices of watermelon lie on a plastic tray atop the washing machine, and an old record player has been pulled out of the storage room. From it comes the voice of a woman who seems to have lost everything.

Bill is trying to read the name on the spinning record when the old man passes by.

"Piaf," he says. "Edith Piaf."

Bill and Sabine step away from the party without really meaning to. He has a plate with nothing on it but a little icing. She has an empty wineglass. It is fall, spring, summer, winter; it makes no difference.

"How is Frankie?"

"Frankie B or Frankie K?"

"Either."

They're walking down Gulf Drive. He throws his plate in a neighbor's garbage can.

"Frankie B got a letter from his lady saying she hopes he gets out soon so she can sue his ass for nonpayment. 'That's some girlfriend,' another guy said, and Frankie said, That's my wife,' and he got in a fight over it, and he's not working in the laundry no more. He said he had an ulcer, but when they couldn't find that, he said it was his tooth that was hurting. I watched him eat all through dinner, though, and he doesn't look like his tooth is hurting."

Her profile has become a fixed shape at the edge of his vision. He stops to inspect it, and she stops, too. This moment before they kiss—of which he will recall only the damp odor of champagne, of which she will recall only the taste of tobacco—this is the oxygen of love.

"What about Frankie K?" she says.

"I don't speak to him anymore."

A little while later, they sit beside the pool with the liver-spotted man between them. The man is going into the hospital in Bradenton tomorrow for an operation.

"They used to have to crack your chest right in half. That's how they did it to my daddy."

"Is that right?" Bill is watching Sabine, who sits across from him avoiding his gaze and sipping from a glass of champagne.

"Now they just go in through the back. I'll be home with my feet up next morning. Peggy? What do they call it?" His daughter, an old woman in her own right, sits nearby, but she either hasn't heard him or chooses not to respond. "Lazaruscopic," he says. "Something like that."

Sabine looks at Bill, then turns to say goodbye to a departing guest.

"That's modern medicine."

THE NEXT WEEK, she forgets her purse at home, and a few blocks before they get to the motel, she turns off the main road. Most of the houses sit out on a dry square of crabgrass, baking in the sun, but the house she shares with Tom is tucked back in a huddle of trees and vines and banana plants, almost purple in its shadow. Bill follows her up the walk, and steps after her into the house's cool, dark air.

The front hall is narrow and dark. No lights are on, and the only sound is a fan running in the room beyond. A black-and-white cat prances out of an unseen hall and frisks about their ankles.

She goes upstairs to hunt for her purse, and he looks around, trying to decide what is Tom's and what's hers. The collection of *National Geographics*, the paperweight with flakes of gold suspended in its mass, the walnut end table: these must belong to the husband. But the dried-up orchid, the coffee cup of highlighters, the tear-off calendar: these can only be Sabine's. Hers, too, would be the photographs of cruise-ship cabins, and the photogravures of stern-looking Prussian women and of boys on ice skates. He feels a kind of kinship with Tom, the way one looking out across the ocean feels kinship with the person they imagine on the opposite shore. *Is it raining over there? Has he had lunch?*

Getting himself a glass of water from the sink, he thinks of all the times she has done exactly this. Picked up the glass, felt the water cool her palm as it is filled. The room is alive with her having touched it. He looks in the dishwasher. He hefts a remote control in his hand. At the far end of the room are a door, half-open, and a desk and bookshelf. It is maybe there that she writes his letters, and her whole life seems to him as near and knowable as the contents of that room. He longs to spend five minutes in her closet, to flush the toilets and interrogate the cat. The cat, sitting with his nose nearly touching the glass doors, watching a sparrow on the patio, his tail twitched by the delicate recollection of feathers on the tongue—he must be hers.

She stands at the top of the steps with her purse under her arm, simply listening to the sound of the man loitering in her living room. What is she listening for? She doesn't know and doesn't need to.

THE DAY HAS turned hot by the time they get to the motel, and by the pool, they find the lounge chairs filled with guests: a little girl missing her front teeth; a biker with a neck on which thorned tattoos are nearly invisible beneath the sunburn; a sleeping woman with her mouth open. The sun sits high and pompous over the afternoon, and Bill gathers up used towels and dumps them in a pile for Britta. Sabine goes to check in a couple from Alaska, and then she carries an armful of linens up to the honeymoon suite and finds Bill there, lying with his eyes closed on the tile floor.

They say nothing as they tumble toward the bed. It is as though they've memorized the same equation. Sweat burns in his eyes. She lies beside him. He might kiss her forehead or her elbow, but instead he breathes out and lets his thoughts loll. He thinks it has begun to rain, but when he looks, it hasn't. Sometime later, he reaches out and runs the backs of his fingers down her sternum, but she has fallen asleep, goes on dreaming, remains far away, as unreal to him as you are to me.

THE NEXT SATURDAY, he pesters her without end—follows her from the office to the laundry, the laundry to the store-room, saying she's beautiful, saying he can't live without her—and she is sure at any minute Tom will walk around the corner. She swats away his hand again and again but then, in a hallway, allows him to trace the line of her neck with kisses. He begs her to meet him, anywhere, anytime, he only wants to see her, to talk to her. She doesn't say no, because she doesn't want to give him the satisfaction of an answer, and because she isn't sure she could make it sound as though she meant it. But after lunch she relents and, carrying an extra set of linen, goes to wait for him in the second-floor suite. Now he dallies. He asks Britta about her childhood, talks with Tom about the gutters, sticks pieces of grass in the parrot's cage. When he can think of absolutely nothing else to do, he runs up the stairs. The room is half-dark, the curtains drawn, and his eyes have not adjusted when from the bed she tells him to bolt the door, as if he doesn't know to do this already. He tries to take off all his clothes at once.

How do they see themselves in this moment? They take this passion as proof of their need for each other. If nothing else, they have this. Bill thinks of it as harmless fun, and knowing—how could he not—that this represents for him a fantastic alteration of circumstances, he begins to embroider his visions of parole with acts of fornication and porterhouse steaks. Sabine feels returned to some younger version of herself, made almost a girl again.

They change the sheets—she on one side of the bed, he on the other—and when they leave and close the door behind them, the room looks as though nothing has happened.

THE WEEKS PASS. The spring begins to warm. It's been well over a month now since the bookseller arrived for the convention in Sarasota. The conventioneers have long since packed up their things and departed, but the bookseller remains. In plaid trunks, he lounges by the pool with a copy of *Ulysses* open on his lap, waiting for someone to walk by and ask him about Leopold Bloom. For the first few weeks, he'd made up excuses about his delayed departure. He had to become increasingly cunning; a person can have only so many mix-ups with the airline, so many canceled flights. One day, he declared he was done with air travel. He'd be taking the train home instead, though—terribly inconvenient— he'd been asked to look over the holdings of a certain private collector first. Who? He gave out a smile of secrets beyond secrets and ran his hand over the faint beginnings of a goatee.

The truth, which he has learned better than to consider, is that he would rather die than return to Binghamton. He has fallen in love with this little motel, and when he thinks of his home, the halls choked with books and the mantels shouldered with dust, he can follow the brick path up, he can put a hand on the front door, but he cannot open it. And anyway, how much more lively to stay on and uncover the ties that bind this odd troupe of characters together. He is charmed by Britta, who seems to him a figure out of a Thomas Mann novel, cast perpetually in a clean forest light. He finds Tom inscrutable. And Bill is just the sort of lighthearted rogue a picaresque requires. Sabine awes him. She blows through the motel with an Übermensch will. He has a volume of Bartram's *Travels* that he plans to bestow upon her when he leaves, though he has yet to ascertain her feelings about rare books. It would be a shame to waste so fine a specimen on one who hadn't developed the faculties to appreciate it, he thinks, but then, recalling a line from Least Heat-Moon, he reminds himself that the value of a gift derives from its dearness not to the recipient but to the giver. And having settled the matter again (already he has had this conversation with himself a number of times; it is a very fine Bartram) and feeling ennobled by the grandeur of this uncommitted act, he drapes a towel over his eyes and drifts into dreams.

It is from these dreams that he is roused by the unmistakable, energetic sound of coitus. He lifts the towel and finds Tom standing just a few feet away, staring fixedly up at the door of the honeymoon suite.

"Ah, Thomas," says the bookseller. "Love, love on a spring night. The cotton lace of her nightgown, the fresh perfume . . ."

The little man remains unmoving and the bookseller decides perhaps a different tack is in order.

"I was just saying to your wife that Lord Byron himself could not have asked for—"

This anecdote, a favorite which never fails to elicit chuckles and adulation, and which he knows to be a particularly delicious little mot juste, is a rather dramatic allusion to the travails of one of literature's great heroes, but he is cut short by the sight of Tom's face, which is now looking at Sabine as she exits the upstairs suite. Before the bookseller can go on, Tom strides to the office and slams the door.

12: Homecoming

WEARING A HAIRNET AND a frayed gray apron, Bill works his morning shift in the mess, and out of nothing more than water and white powder, he creates a beige glue that could almost be mistaken for mashed potatoes. He has a motherly sort of feeling for his fellow inmates and is liberal with the salt. In the afternoons, he works out, a series of stretches and exercises he learned from watching his father, and on Tuesdays and Thursdays, he puts on a pair of donated black-rimmed glasses and attends typing classes. The classes are taught by a former accountant serving a ten-month sentence for wire fraud. The men are given a sheet of paper with certain patterns of letters and symbols, and without looking at the keyboard, they are supposed to replicate the pattern. Sometimes the letters arrange themselves in ways that suggest fragments of words—*flor, proc, decl, ing, into, abra*—and for no reason that he can understand, Bill always associates these occurrences with Sabine.

At night, he brings a book back to his cell. He has not yet discovered the books of George R. R. Martin, and so it is a Western novel he often carries with him. From the time he lies down until the lights go out, he follows the story of a hero wandering along the Mexican border, leaving behind him shot-up Main Streets and the graves of villains. When the lights flick out, Bill turns down the corner on his page and puts the book aside, and then he lies perfectly still on his back. Now, with the prison in the hold of night, the coughs and wheezes of the other inmates come to him from another world far removed from his own. The past weeks are compressed into a frenzied strobe-like story that comes all at once to a grating halt over the memory of her body, and lying quietly on his back, his thoughts drifting over her as a haze drifts above water, he slips into a deep and harmless sleep.

One morning, he awakes and it's the day of his release. With his belongings in a paper bag beneath one arm, he steps through the chain-link fence into a parking lot blurred with heat. It's the final day of August. Sabine stands with her arms crossed and her hip against the door of the car, wearing one of those light cotton dresses that make one think everything will be all right.

"What are you smiling about?" he says, and they nearly topple together into the open convertible.

Wind, blown north from the Caribbean, swings the streetlights over the empty intersections. It tugs at the perms of the elderly women on the tennis courts and clears the sky of clouds.

After a few quick turns, they are out on the highway, the top down, tearing along. He places a hand on her thigh and finds it warm from the sun. The wind is deafening.

"Where to?" she says.

He shrugs. He has absolutely no idea.

"Hungry?"

"I could eat."

They've come to a light. It's still early in the morning. The day hasn't yet made up its mind. There are no other cars to be seen. She puts on her turn signal, and this act brings up in him a feeling he has often had while reading her letters. Neither of them knows where they're going.

"Thanks for getting me," he says, but she doesn't hear. The light has turned green, and the motor howls to life, and as the road swings around and straightens out ahead of them, it no longer seems important.

They spend the day aimlessly. Breakfast in a diner where the waitresses tap their computer screens with long fingernails curved like corn chips. They browse the lot at a used-car dealer. Coffee and juice in the afternoon at a roadside shack, where one wall opens up on the highway like an eye. Then an abrupt turn for the Gulf, and they stop at a tiki bar, where they drink something full of tequila and coconut. She tells him about the place she's rented for them: how perfect it is, how she found just the right color for the walls, just the right couch for the living room. It never occurs to him until they pull up alongside the apartment and he sees the string lights glittering through the bushes that maybe she has been wasting away this day on purpose.

They sit in the car and look at the crowd on the patio. A hand-lettered banner hangs between two palms: WELCOME HOME BILL!! No one but Sabine could have made it.

"Britta helped. She has such nice pens."

"Just steer me toward the fridge," says Bill.

PRISON PREPARES A person for many things, but a cock-tail party is a test all its own. Sabine whispers in Bill's ear the name of each guest, and he repeats the names to himself while looking at their faces. Holding containers of raw asparagus are the Greevys, Ellen and Chuck, both retired from public schools in Minnesota. At the table near them stands Britta, and beside her another German, Karin, reads the labels on the food.

"Eck," says Karin without uncrossing her arms. "Why do they call it German potato salad? We do not have this in Germany."

On the other side of the table is Sabine's trainer, Armando, who has been roped into conversation by Roberta Smith, Tess's mother, the director of the local theater. ("A volunteer position," says Karin.)

Roberta sweeps her arm to take in the table, the guests, the world. "A feast!"

There are other guests—an orthopedic surgeon in seersucker shorts, and his mother; a number of loud Australians; a failed stand-up comedian; a few small children running after one an-other, as there always are at these parties.

Bill spends the first hour excusing himself from one conversa-tion or another to use the restroom, and once there, he looks at his face in the mirror and fingers the bottle caps in the pocket of his jeans. But at some moment—maybe it is the alcohol—the party begins to find a rhythm. Like an orchestra tunes its instruments, the crowd finds its register, and to the surprise of everyone, Bill most of all, it ceases to be an obligation. Armando wraps Britta in his long brown arms and two-steps her across the flagstones. Karin reappears (when had she left?) with a bag of ice, a bag of limes, and a blender. From nowhere, a pink-and-yellow donkey piñata appears on a table, and the two children, a boy and a girl, emerge instantly from the shadows to ask what's in it.

"It's full of little candies," says Karin.

"I bet it's full of rubbers."

"Shush, Roberta."

"I think it's full of kittens," Bill says, and wanders off in the direction of the food.

He catches sight of Sabine on his way. She is coming out of the kitchen, holding a cake in both hands. She has cut her hair still shorter, and it gives her a schoolboyish look. There is a resolve in her movements, in the way she strides through the hedges, and it makes him love to watch her.

"William," says Ellen. "We're talking about France. Have you ever been?"

Before Bill can say anything, there is a thump behind him, and they are showered in candy.

"Little candies!" says Karin with a bat in her hand, while the children anxiously gather the sweets off the ground.

THE PARTY IS nearly over. Brie fused to a plastic cutting board, soft green grapes scattered across the pavers, crackers and stale bread, maroon cocktail napkins crumpled around shrimp tails and a knife crusted with white frosting in the bushes. Ellen is explaining the Israeli-Palestinian conflict to no one in particular while Armando nods off in a chair. Britta gathers the paper plates and puts them in the trash. Inside the apartment, a little girl sleeps on the couch, her hand hanging limply into a potted geranium. The stars are out, but only Roberta sees them.

Finally, the last guests are leaving. The Greevys stand wavering just inside the door, a little like apparitions, a little like drunks.

"We're socialists," he says.

She swats him on the arm. "Don't say that. It was lovely to meet you, William."

Chuck is trying to goad his wife along, but she keeps weaving out from beneath his hands and coming up with something else to say. He wavers over the face of his watch.

"My god, it's three in the morning, Ellie. Let these poor people sleep."

"All right, let's go," she says. "Where's my jacket?"

They are on the threshold. Now, suddenly, the husband remembers something he had wanted to mention.

"Really do come by and see us."

"Four-oh-four Willow," the wife adds. "Palm trees out front."

Arm in arm, they march out into the dark and disappear, only to reappear again briefly, as if to threaten one final goodbye, beneath the streetlamp on the corner.

Now Bill closes the door and, thinking of those two final guests, locks it with a flourish. Sabine, lying on the couch beneath a yellow slicker, already almost asleep, her head held up by her hand, calls him.

"Here," she says.

Out from between the couch cushions she produces a small box wrapped in silver paper and pushes it into his hands.

Inside, sandwiched between two thin layers of polyester wool, is a heavy silver watch. Its face is blank except for twelve very faintly filigreed Roman numerals and, in the center, a word, in German maybe, that he doesn't recognize. He has never worn a watch, and he needs her help to put it on. He leans dramatically over the watch face.

"My god, it's three in the morning, Ellie."

She laughs softly, and softly rests her head on her arm.

Now it has been a long day. They remove their clothes, brush their teeth, wash their faces, moving through the motions as ones lost already to sleep. She takes off her earrings. He runs a hand through his hair. They seem to be following around an image of themselves.

"Did I already say, 'Welcome home'?" she asks. "Or did I only think it?"

13: The Confidence of Friends

IT'S FULL MORNING WHEN he wakes. Two weeks have passed, and he wakes not to an alarm but to the beeps of a dump truck backing up on the next street over. With his eyes still closed, the room spins around like a compass needle until it settles into its geography. Some rag of dream pursues him out of sleep, a feeling more than anything, but even as he opens his eyes, it's already gone.

He lies in a wide blue bed, and turning his head, he finds the still-sleeping profile of Sabine. With her nose up and a soft snore escaping from her parted lips, she seems to him to be scenting the air for news. Beside him, the watch lies on the night table. He feels as though the person who received it was another man in another life. He inspects it closely, this silver watch with the round white face. It's not yet eight o'clock. For the first time in a while, he feels the natural goodwill and generosity of the well slept. He slips from beneath the sheets and moves away from the bed with stealth and tenderness.

With the money he'd saved up in work release, he's rented a storage unit halfway down the island and filled it with a rotary saw, a workbench, and a secondhand sander. The room is ten feet by fifteen. He has to heave up the blue metal door with two hands. He always leaves this door open when he works. Across the road, he can see the Gulf. No one uses the other units much. Sometimes a young man comes on the weekend and loads his pickup with large plastic tubs of fishing gear and tackle, but otherwise he has the view to himself.

He'd found a miniature refrigerator that wasn't being used at the motel, and he keeps this stocked with blue-and-gold cans of malt liquor. The first thing he does when he comes down here, even before flicking on the light, is to reach into the frosted back of the fridge and pull out one of these cans. The first sip cools the air of the storage unit. He leans against the workbench and pushes his sunglasses up on his head, and once he's finished the first beer, he goes around plugging in the machines and dusting things off.

He doesn't know how to describe to Sabine the way he feels at these times, the ownership he feels of this space, and the familiarity of it. The screech of the saw and the electrical shocks given him by the sander. The way his cans have a little cuff of yellow sawdust around their bottoms. Drinking is as necessary a part of the operation as is the hammer. It makes him feel calm. The saw spins of its own accord, the fan sends waves of dust spiraling out into the parking lot, and he watches as a bench takes shape beneath his hands.

When Sabine arrives, appearing in the open door, he kisses her and covers her in sawdust.

They talk awhile about nothing in particular. He shows her the things he is working on, and explains the work still to be done. On her way out, she brushes the dust from her jeans and glances into the trash. After that, he begins to put his empties directly in the Dumpster.

ONE NIGHT NOT long after this, while he's asleep, she takes all the beer out of the refrigerator and pours it in the sink. In the morning, she lies in bed and listens. He goes to the fridge first, and there's a long silence after the door opens. Then it closes very softly. He rummages around the apartment, then the refrigerator opens again and closes with a smack, and he begins counting the empties in the recycling. After a while, the apartment goes silent. She lies still in the dark bedroom and listens to a hedge trimmer in the neighbor's yard, and after a while, she realizes he's standing in the doorway watching her. She turns over and smiles at him.

"Come back to bed."

"Very funny."

IN THE BATHROOM at dusk, with two fingers, he picks up a hand towel stained with mascara and tries to remove the specks of flossed-out broccoli from the mirror. A cotton swab lies in the shower water on the floor, a few inches from the wastebasket, but he cannot bring himself to touch it. He dawdles in the bathroom. Everything he does here, he does slowly. He treasures these small privacies. The day has been searing, and the shower seems to break the heat. When she finally arrives from work, she paces outside the door. He's going to make them late, she reminds him.

He is still running the towel over his head when she bursts in. In the bathroom, she does everything at once. She brushes her teeth in the shower, and rinses her mouth while clipping her nails. The only time she is ever still is when she sits on the toilet; elbows on knees and chin in hands, she is like a bird-watcher or a little child learning about the solar system. He loiters in the doorway. She frowns and waves him away. Even more than his own, he enjoys the privacy of others.

They have a drink before they leave, and he remembers what it is to be in love, to think about a cigarette, watch your beer be poured, swat away a fly. To watch her and have her look up, this is wonderful, but how much more wonderful to watch her without her ever realizing. He feels as though he owns a piece of her that she herself can't even see. She opens his beer absentmindedly. She sighs, puts the bottle cap in the trash, and grimaces at whatever smell she meets with there. He could say something—he half wishes she would look up—but instead he looks back down at the newspaper and pretends to be reading, but he continues every so often to let his eyes rise above the page and linger on her.

They drive along the Gulf toward Sarasota, past Holmes Beach, Bradenton Beach, Coquina Beach. The road is sinewy at night. The car runs the curves as if on tracks. He drags a hand through the evening air, and little bugs swim up, flash death-white in the headlights, and are gone.

At the restaurant, the valet attendants are clustered in the entryway in polo shirts, and as Bill and Sabine pass through the open door, there is the sound of wineglasses being put away. A piano plays in another room. Bottles of liquor are ranged on shelves behind the bar all the way to the ceiling. The walls are covered in corks. The host wears a tidy blue suit and a mustache. He looks over their heads as though checking to see there is not someone more important behind them.

"Four," Bill says.

"Name?"

Bill looks to Sabine.

"Musil-Buehler."

As they enter the dining room, they see the Greevys already at the table, sitting together quietly, having run out of things to say to each other. In the corner, a blind pianist leans on his cane between sets, asking a busgirl for a ginger ale.

"Don't you look sharp," Ellen says to Bill, and Chuck laughs.

Like the corn that so engrosses their native Midwest, the Greevys are dry and rattling husks, but how redeemed are these two by the abracadabra of scotch whiskey. Already as the waiter approaches with two glasses on a tray, Chuck Greevy's cheeks flush red, and Ellen Greevy lets out a high horsey chuckle at some forgettable remark.

"There is nothing sadder in the whole world than a stray cat that's gotten itself knocked up," says Ellen. She has just finished a term as the treasurer of the SPCA.

"It's terrible," says Sabine.

"A procedure that costs hardly more than an entrée."

"My pop," Bill says, "he just got a bucket of warm water when the cat's time came."

Sabine looks at him with her lips pressed together.

"That's one way," says Ellen.

"The cat got sneaky, though. She had her last litter in the ceiling."

"It is astounding, isn't it?" Chuck says to Bill. "The pure stubborn will of life."

"My husband has gotten very profound since his last prostate exam."

Chuck holds up his thumb and forefinger. "This close to becoming a eunuch."

"A eunuch, sir?"

"Impotent," says Sabine.

"It can be a very emasculating procedure," Ellen says to Bill. "Have you had your prostate checked?"

"I believe in a higher power," says Chuck.

"Well, there has to be something," Bill says to Sabine. "Otherwise, why did everything begin?"

"I am interested," Chuck Greevy says, signaling a waiter for another scotch. "I'm interested in the deep correspondences between—"

In a flourish of white sleeves, the appetizers arrive.

Carrots have been cut into diamonds and stacked on top of one another. Bill pushes the pile over with his fork, but there is nothing underneath it.

"Oh, gracious," says Ellen. After a drink or two, she sometimes adopts this Southern air. "Marcus performs miracles with a vegetable."

Dinner goes on like this. Sabine, Chuck, and Ellen seem to be having one conversation. Bill is having another. Eventually, he gives up talking and excuses himself to the bar. When he returns,

Sabine's eyes look once at his face. She doesn't look at him again during dinner.

THAT NIGHT, THE stars are out. The ocean is like a great fallow field. He had wanted to drive, but she wouldn't let him. He looks down the streets as they go by and counts the seconds for no good reason. She steers with the heel of one palm.

At the apartment, she puts on music and opens a bottle of wine. He turns on the air conditioner.

"I'm chilly," she says, and they pass the rest of the night in silence. Around midnight, he goes out to smoke, and she's in bed when he comes back in. He washes his hands and gets in beside her, and for a long time neither of them sleeps.

What was it they had expected to find in each other? She is a vegetarian. He eats meat. She has never smoked a cigarette in her life. He smoked one before brushing his teeth that night. They both love French fries, convertibles, Frank Sinatra, lying on the beach, but he can lie all day on the sand and she gets antsy after fifteen minutes. Neither of them is a good swimmer, but only he is afraid of drowning. She reads books, does crosswords, makes lists. Books remind him of prison. Her dreams are vivid and theatrical: limousines that stretch kilometers on end, animals that discourse on topics elaborate and mundane, lavish banquets where all the guests are ugly, rich, and bronze. When his dreams do settle into scenery, it's usually a familiar place: a certain trailer from his childhood, the room where he has gone to sleep, a windowless cell. The light is always dim, and he feels nervous, as though waiting for the neighbors to begin fighting.

When they wake the next day, whatever it was has passed. An

argument, maybe. It's not worth thinking about. She smiles at him from the across the bed. The morning spills in rapid gold across her pillow. He has a headache, and feeling like a holy man alone on a mountain, he takes two aspirin and is penitent. They kiss, and they know that they were not meant to be unhappy. How could they have forgotten. It's so simple now that it's hard to understand how it could ever have been otherwise. He kisses her on the ear.

Out at the beach, he lies on the sand like a dog, and like a dog he is content. She reads the newspaper. His head is in her lap. A seagull's shadow passes across his closed eyes. The spine of the paper snaps inward in the wind. Some voices drift down to them from a family far off up the beach. She is holding the paper in one hand. The other, without thinking about it, she runs through his hair.

EACH DAY RIPENS slowly—a few clouds shaped like horses out along the horizon; the smell of charcoal, shrimp, and kerosene; the wheeze of her bicycle behind him; cut grass on a sidewalk; the birds and flowers with names he can't remember; his tiptoeing while she sleeps; a boy walking home from school with a pack banging at the backs of his knees; breezes bouncing house to house down the street; a dream of sharks; her voice on the telephone in the other room; a vertiginous hovering above a urinal; the ringing of car keys; the rubber smell of her skin after a workout and the blue T-shirt spongy with sweat; rough men with bright hooks, fishing from the pier; the bridge to St. Petersburg just visible across the bay like the skeleton of a dinosaur—till at dusk, in a circling of birds, it all fillips into evening and is gone.

It is the middle of the night. He doesn't remember waking, but here he is. The windows are open, and a breeze moves the curtains. Maybe half an hour he lies there, wondering if he'll fall back to sleep. He gets up, uses the bathroom, goes and opens the door to the patio, and stands in the doorway. The sky has not begun to lighten. The island is quiet. The wind picks up, and as if the palms have been trying to tell him something, he realizes it's going to rain. No sooner does he think it than the first drops arrive, not visibly but as a hush, coming in from the Gulf and bringing in the scent of wet paper, canvas, pavement, lime. The hush gathers itself into a grumble, and at last the rain plangs on the gutters and the leaves, and begins to splotch the patio. The shower gains strength without ever seeming to. The water falls gently but with persistence, sending up a light drumming from the cars in the lot. His feet are flecked with rain, and reaching out beyond the eaves, he rinses his hands. Two months have passed since his release: he has no job, no friends, no money. Looking back, what is there?

They have accustomed to each other, and they go around all day attended by the usual joys and miseries. He waits for her at home, lusting, tidying, and lusting once more, but when she finally arrives, he has no interest in her. They begin to excel at disagreements. It is as though they now occupy two diametrically opposed worlds. If he is hot, she is cold. If he is tired, she is ready to clean the apartment. If he tries to kiss her on a street corner, she turns away.

SHE'S NOT AT the motel, so he goes looking for her at her house. She answers the door in a dress.

"You can't be here," she says.

"What are you all dressed up for?"

"Tom said he'll call the police if he sees you here."

He scratches the stubble on his throat and sniffs.

"Bill," she says. "You have to leave."

He doesn't leave, and they end up sitting in the kitchen and talking. He is trying to explain to her about how Tom is coming between them, about the stress.

"What stress?"

"The stress! I got a whole wheelbarrow full of stress!"

At seven, she starts to gather her things, and he watches her and looks out the window. The sun is setting, and the vacationers across the canal are trying to light their grill.

"You're not going to invite me along?" he says.

THEY BEGIN TO fall apart on Halloween. The day is warm, breezy. Dolphins are still jumping and shimmering out in the breakers, but bales of straw and pumpkins have been set up outside of the grocery stores. Bill and Sabine wake before ten to the sound of first graders parading down the block: superheroes, princesses, witches, goblins, a sheep, a dog, a zombie, a child who appears to have no costume at all. At the very end comes the gym teacher, in gray running shorts, gathering the dropped tiaras, the vampire teeth, the clown noses, the severed finger.

It is Sabine's favorite holiday. She is to spend the day decorating the motel.

"What time should I come over?" he says.

"Oh," she says. "Some other people are helping to set things up. You don't need to worry about it."

"Who?" he says.

KARIN AND BRITTA are stretching cobwebs around the trunks of the palms that afternoon when Bill shows up holding a pumpkin.

"You're drunk," Sabine says.

"Don't worry," he says and sits down by the pool. "I'm not going to help. You don't need my help, so I'm just going to sit here and carve this pumpkin."

But he never carves the pumpkin. He looks at it for a while, and when Britta passes by, he tells her how good it's going to be, how they're going to put a picture of this pumpkin in a magazine when he's done with it. Then he sits and watches Armando putting up plywood gravestones. When Sabine finally asks if he could give her a hand, he jumps out of his seat.

"Now you want my help?" He points at Armando. "Get him to help." And he storms off down the street, still carrying his pumpkin.

"Leave him," Karin says to Sabine.

"What will he do?"

"Not your problem."

"What do you think, Britta?"

"He doesn't seem very stable," Britta says.

"He's dangerous," says Karin.

"What if you talked to him?" Britta says. "What if you told him you weren't happy?"

Karin purses her lips and looks out across the road. Tom passes by with a werewolf head.

"Leave," Karin says. "It's as simple as that."

THE WINDOW IS large and full of plants. The light comes in green and sour. There's a chime on the door. The room smells of sweat, nylon, and patchouli. Armando, the trainer, shares the space with a yoga studio. He'll have his own place soon, without the gong in the corner, without the chakras on the wall.

He rubs Sabine down at the end of the hour, as he rubs all his girls. His hands enliven the flesh. It is why they come back, to be rubbed and to talk about what they are capable of.

"You can do that!" he says.

"Don't you think I'm too—"

"Don't you say too old. Never too old."

"But—"

"Girl, you do whatever you want. You tell him who's the boss. You got the looks. You got the money. What's he got? If I was you, I just go. Not tell him. Go down to Puerto Rico. Take your girlfriends and have a nice time."

Of course his clients tell him everything: affairs, addictions, bad dreams and bad mortgages. And he remembers almost none of it. He doesn't gossip but has only a passing interest in their stories.

"Oh my god," he says. "It's two. I got to go. I got a date."

THE AFTERNOON IS strangely cool and temperate, a slack wind blowing in to shore. The sun dives behind each passing cloud, and the beach is mostly empty. Guests come into the office looking for museum brochures. December feels nearer than anyone had hoped.

Each hour of the afternoon seems to drag on forever, promising that one is appointed to a thousand future obligations of equal dullness. Tom spins side to side in his chair and dreams about boats, shuffling things around on the desk as if busy. He imagines a Boston Whaler with varnished oak along the keel, a blue gunwale, and stripes of red and gold running the length of the hull. Or maybe a trim little sailboat, all white, tacking up the coast with him at the rudder, in white, as well. There is the hint of a beautiful woman belowdecks. Every few minutes, he checks his watch and looks out the door mournfully.

He carries these daydreams home with him, but even a beer and a rest in the hammock can't dispel the tedium. He sweeps the patio, spends some time staring down into the canal and rubbing the back of his neck. The task of preparing dinner seems insurmountable, and an image looms up of an open box of pizza and the glare of the TV reflected in the patio doors. How long he has been standing in the kitchen, he can't say. He is pulled from the reverie by the sound of Sabine's tires rolling into the drive. He looks up at the same time as the cat.

Sabine flops onto the couch, and as the cat runs to her, Tom wants to say something, but he doesn't know what. She sits up.

"Can you make some room in the garage?" she says. "I may move a few things back."

THE APARTMENT ON Magnolia Avenue sits nearly empty. A few dishes are in the sink. An old banana sends up its stink from a bowl on the counter, and two fruit flies zigzag drowsily above it. Otherwise, there is hardly anything there. The past few days, without mentioning it to Bill, Sabine has been removing her things from the drawers. Her toothbrush lies on its side by the bathroom sink, but almost everything else is gone. Everything Bill owns is in the apartment, but that doesn't amount to much: a pair of boots, a stack of new white undershirts, the watch. He has no photos of family, no family rings, no pens, no diary. No books on the nightstand. In his wallet, there are no lists—not of things to do, not of numbers to call in case of emergency. Neither are there credit cards, insurance cards, business cards. There are two dollars and a crumpled wad of receipts. He has no shampoo of his own. He has no dress shoes, no Swiss Army knife, no son to give it to. Where now are his arrowhead collection, his grandpa's purple rabbit-foot? Where is the jean jacket he wore as a little boy? If, as Borges says, things are what marry us to the world, what can one make of this dearth? On top of Bill's dresser, there is nothing but a mirror and a pack of cigarettes.

14: A Disagreement

THE LIQUOR STORE IS as cold as a vault, and the old man, the owner, sits on a high stool behind the counter, looking down on everyone who enters. From a speaker in the back, a few watery lines of Ella Fitzgerald drift into the room. When a woman in a sun hat asks a question, he jumps down and hobbles over to her. There is something wrong with his legs, a deformity that has marked him since youth, now as much a part of his temperament as of his body. His disdainful gaze barely comes level with the woman's breasts, and pulling a pair of eyeglasses down from his head, he peers at the bottle of wine she's holding.

"Beaujolais, Beaujolais, Beaujolais," he says. "Beaujolais is all the same."

He makes his way back to the counter and climbs again onto

his stool and sits there, staring out the window. The woman buys the bottle anyway. His is the only store on the island. She thanks him and leaves, and his eyes follow her across the parking lot until a white convertible drives up.

Sabine walks across the asphalt. She wears sneakers, jeans, a flowered shirt with the sleeves rolled up. Her legs are long, and she's in no hurry. He once heard her speak against property taxes at a city council meeting—her jaw clenching, a slight nervousness in her voice. He's adored her ever since.

"*Wilkommen, meine Frau.*"

"Freddie." She nods and passes by, dragging his gaze along behind her.

He trails her around the store, showing her first this bottle, then that one. She smells just barely of sweat, and he inhales this scent and thinks of crushed grapes. The big front window is covered in a brown plastic film. Through it, the sun shines like a burning penny, filling the store with a deep caramel gloom. He limps behind her through the mountains of Bavaria, the hot, dry plains of southern Spain, the fortress towns of Tuscany with their dank crypts in which a pair of middle-aged lovers might casually embrace.

She dallies. She has no interest in anything particular. She wants only something cold and white to drink while watching television, but she feels compelled to delay the decision. Anyway, she doesn't mind listening to Freddie go on about vintages and crus, and it's pleasant to hold the expensive bottles he keeps placing in her hands. When she turns away, he undoes one of the buttons on his shirt, and a minute later, he redoes it. He would give it all up, every bit, to picnic with her someday in Sonoma.

At last, she picks a pinot grigio off the discount shelf.

He doesn't wince. "An excellent choice," he says. "Good value. My wife, may she rest in peace, drank chardonnay." He puts his hand over his chest. "I prefer verdicchio."

That she would have picked another bottle. Here is an excellent champagne, there a near-perfect Barolo. She could have afforded them. He would gladly have given them to her. But now it's too late. Freddie has slipped the bottle into a paper sleeve, and as he rests it in her palm, he lets his hairy hand brush her arm. She leaves. He sighs. And so, on the last night of her life, Sabine drinks pinot grigio.

It hasn't yet begun to darken when she pulls up at the apartment. She gathers her things, and as she walks across the terrace, lizards scatter over the cement. Bill isn't home. The apartment is quiet. She puts a bag of groceries on the counter and stands in the middle of the kitchen with the wine in her hand not looking at anything in particular. She hasn't thought the words yet, but somewhere in her mind she's begun to think that she'll be better off without him. Her whole body has loosened. You can see it in the way she walks, a languor and abandon. She turns on the TV and heads for the shower, where she lets the hot water run until she can hardly see herself in the steam.

The lizards have just emerged again, clustering in a rhombus of sunlight on the wall, when Bill walks into the lot and sends them darting back into the shadows. He sees her car and looks in the window without much reason. When he enters the house, the groceries still sit on the counter in their plastic bag, her sneakers are in the middle of the room, the shower is running, the bottle of wine is open on the counter. He knows that something is going to happen, though he can't tell what.

She stays a long time in the shower. The water is so hot it flushes her skin red. Her palms wrinkle, and she imagines, as she used to when she was a girl, that she is breathing the thick air of a jungle. The closing of the door to the apartment and the opening of the fridge, these sounds come to her as from another life.

Wrapped in a towel, she stands steaming in the middle of the bathroom. Her face in the fogged mirror is the face of women glimpsed in subway stations, at the parties of strangers, through the window of cafés, arresting, undefined. She has the sensation that she could wipe away the years as easily as the fog, and she hums and slowly rubs her skin with some lotion smelling of lavender and honey, which she spent too much money on.

Though the apartment is small, they manage to avoid each other for a time. She is in the bathroom combing her wet hair, and as she comes out, he goes into the kitchen and begins looking through the bags of groceries. When he finishes, she has her head in a cupboard, and he goes directly to the bedroom and lays himself out for a few minutes on the bed.

"Are you hungry?" she says to the empty kitchen.

His murmur is too faint to be a yes.

It's not time yet, but he winds the watch. She doesn't go in to get her book from the nightstand until she hears him enter the bathroom. They meet at last on the couch, she at one end with a book, he at the other.

But now that she sees their relationship as a temporary state, it's much easier to get along. They are like lovers removed by years from an affair. She has her feet tucked beneath her. He stretches out his arms and legs, and yawns. Cordial and polite, pensive with recollected desire, they listen avidly as the other speaks.

"The oldest little couple," she says. "They looked just like, just like two raisins. Exactly identical. You couldn't tell the difference, except he was bald, completely bald, with a shine on the top."

He grins and sips his beer.

"They asked for the honeymoon suite," she says. "I wish you could have seen them."

They run out of things to say, but neither of them moves. It is as though they are waiting for directions. He looks out the window. A car pulls into the parking lot, then turns around and goes back the way it came. She flips through her book, reading pieces here and there, but the meaning escapes her. The words run out from under her eyes, and she closes the book and lets her foot rest on his thigh. He looks with fascination at her toes, then between them.

"It tickles," she says. They end up in bed.

WHEN THEY WAKE, the apartment is dark. They stumble out into the black rooms, first him, then her. Only the light above the stove is on, and it seems to place in relief all that is meager and paltry in their life together. The half-empty bottle of wine sits in a pool of its own condensation. The discount clothes are thrown in a heap on the chair. Now the bond is dissolved. Something has come between them while they slept, not the resentment of the past days, something more final, less cruel, more distant. Neither turns on a light. He pulls a T-shirt over his head and goes outside.

She sits on the couch in only a bra and underwear and says nothing, does not even look as the back door opens and closes. As soon as he's outside, she gets up and paces the room. She looks at the front door of the apartment. You want to tell her to leave now. There's nothing to gain by confronting him. There's no reward for letting him know. You want to bang on the window, but she can't hear you. The door might as well be locked.

Outside, the little universe of the match illuminates his cupped palms, his tilted face, the skin beneath his eyes, then flashes out. A spurt of smoke shoots up directly at the stars. The night is chilly. The palms chatter in the wind. The boys have gone home with their football to eat hamburgers and macaroni. Outside of beer, he has had nothing all day. His body is hollow, and the smoke, when he inhales it, rubs up against the underside of his skin. His head feels light, and he doesn't realize the cigarette is finished until he's back inside.

When he returns, the television throws a blue glow around the bedroom. He thinks he will duck into the bathroom and brush his teeth before she sees him, but she is waiting there for him. She comes up close to his chest, points her nose at him like a finger, and sniffs.

"Cigarettes?" she says.

"Listen."

But she's already walking away. He follows her to the couch, where she pulls on her shirt and turns her back to him.

"This isn't working," she says.

Why bother recording the arguments of lovers. They are only asking, *Why did I love you?* and that question has no answer. It is an argument about his smoking, a childish habit, and about her behavior, controlling, but it's not about either of those things. He says the things that he's been planning to say, and she does the same, but the wound they make is not what either had expected.

He plants his feet, with his hands at his sides. She sits on the couch, putting on her shoes. In the end, it is only a disagreement about a cigarette. That it had been something grander.

"You know what the problem is," she says, drawing her laces tight with quick jerks of the wrist.

But he has not finished. There are other things he wants to say. He can see everything so clearly right now. If only he could find a way to put it into words. He goes over to her, and so quickly do these things occur, so rapidly does he reach out, that a minute later he will be unable to say what exactly has happened.

WHEN SHE OPENS her eyes, he is above her. The television is on, but she can't hear it. Her mouth tastes bitter.

"You would not believe the headache I have," she tries to say, but her tongue has trouble forming the words. He is very close to her, and he looks frightened, and she realizes—it seems like some sort of joke—his hands are around her neck. "Don't," she says and tries to stand. Instead, so slowly that she can hardly tell what is happening, she slips down onto the floor with him on top of her.

The tile presses against the back of her head, and already any pain has subsided. All of her body now feels cool, a chill very reminiscent of the winters of her childhood, and with great effort, she turns the hand that lies before her and sees there a bluish color gathering beneath the fingernails. There is a fantastic looseness in her limbs, a feeling of liquidity, but she cannot move them. Lying here, in utter relaxation, it is as though she has been cast in marble. For some time, she listens to a wild irregular pattering, without realizing it is her heartbeat. The clapping of the valves is clearer than she has ever heard it, as if the organ itself were a sort of ear.

She tries to gasp a little air, and her nostrils quiver with the effort. How terrible she must look trying to breathe in this fashion, she thinks—like a horse.

She studies herself closely, backing away from her sight until at last she bobs above her body the way a balloon bobs above a mailbox. Looking around, she sees her surroundings still, but now the objects in the room have begun to blur and refract. Each thing trembles with the image of its future. It is charming, this shimmering in time. The table is there, four legs planted firmly on the floor, and yet it hardly seems to be a table. In fact, she can no longer recall the word for it. Bill's face is above her, and she examines it with a great deal of interest. So distorted are his features that for a time she hardly recognizes him. Something seems to be occurring just beneath the surface of his skin, and the muscles in his face are moving as if jerked by strings. He looks very afraid, and she cannot imagine what it is that could frighten him so terribly. And then it ceases to be his face at all. She can't remember who it is. It could be Tom, or a man from very long ago, or another thing entirely, a toaster or a giraffe. She laughs, but her throat is so hot and raw the sound dries to nothing before it leaves her lips.

What was it she was thinking about? She can no longer remember. *I'm having trouble focusing,* she thinks. *I should focus.* But the thoughts lose their edges anyway, soften and come apart. It can't have been that important, after all, if she's forgotten it. The words drift down like bits of snow now. Phrases return to her from conversations long ago, from books she read as a girl, but they have been freed from their origins and meanings. They drift gracefully down, disturbed only barely by the faint wagging of her thought, and finally they aren't disturbed at all.

But a body wants to go on doing forever and ever what it last meant to do. As if to a throne, something is beginning to ascend within her now. A kind of wave runs up along the inside of her spine, grasps her by the inmost fiber and shakes, and she draws in a breath that seems to burst her eyes, and tries to reach down to tie her sneakers. In an instant, she's driven down against the floor by an impossible weight. It presses her through the floor, and she is drawn away again. It is not like giving birth or being born. At the last, it is more like being tipsy, queasy and tipsy, and a good friend with a forlorn face has her by the elbow, is pulling her away, with gentle reassurances and encouragements, from the lights and colors and songs of the party. As her head falls back, she sees on her shirtfront three bright-red drops of blood, and she thinks that now it's ruined.

15: What Lights a Fire

FOR ALL THE FUSS that was made about it, he can't believe how easy it was. It was like she was 101 years old and the good Lord just took her away on home. She murmured something he couldn't hear, and he leaned in closer. "Don't," she said, and she looked up at him like she didn't know who he was, and then she just stopped trying. When her last breath came out and the muscles in her neck went loose, it was like she'd been carrying this weight and she'd finally gotten to put it down.

Now she is lying there with her eyes open, but she isn't moving. He is sitting on the floor a few feet away, though he can't say how he got there. His chest feels like it's bound tight with a belt, and he keeps trying to swallow but can't. He doesn't need to see if she is breathing. She looks peaceful, and if it weren't for the droplets of red across her cheek, he could almost believe she was just lost in thought.

He gets up and walks straight to the bedroom, and strips the sheet from the bed. After laying the sheet out beside her body, he puts her feet together and her arms to her sides, and rolls her up just like a burrito. Only when she is wrapped does he look around to see where he can put her. He settles on the laundry room and drags her down the unlit hall. Now he can think, and he goes to the refrigerator and gets another beer.

He has to think of a plan now. He walks back and forth across the apartment, stopping as he passes the window to look out at the courtyard and the street. He needs to stop looking out the window and think of a plan, but he doesn't. Instead, he stands with the curtain pushed aside and remembers how easy it was, how she didn't resist at all. He looks over to where she was lying with her feet sticking out in the middle of the floor, and he looks down the hall at the closed door to the laundry room, and out the window. Someone walks by, and he whips the curtain closed. He can still see her face like it had been, not even looking at him, and can still feel the way her whole body just went slack, and he just can't believe how easy it was. He puts down the beer beside the couch and studies his hands.

There are a dozen beers in the fridge. He's got to figure a way to paint a picture like he didn't do what he did, but he has to calm down first. So he opens another beer. He didn't really do it anyway. He did, but that's not how it feels. He doesn't feel like he could have killed her. He walks down the hall and peeks in the laundry room, just to make sure. She's still lying there in the dark, so he closes the door again, softly, and locks it.

When he pokes his head out into the courtyard, he expects the neighbor to be out walking her little dog, but the street is empty, and only Sabine's car is in the lot. The apartment door closes, and a moment later, it opens again. Bent over, he steps backward through the doorway, and with a yank to get it over the threshold, the rolled-up sheet emerges after him. He drags her with little steps across the courtyard and out to the car. The trunk is full of her things, so he runs around to the driver's-side door and moves the seat all the way forward. As he tries to push her into the back seat, he is overcome by a feeling of remove, like somebody else is doing everything, and he is merely watching. He sees his hands shoving at the fabric and hears himself cursing under his breath, but he has no power to stop himself from doing these things. He pushes her into the car up to her waist, but then her shoulder gets jammed against something, so he goes around to the other side and pulls on her from there until he has her half folded on the seat with her face down in one corner and her rear end up in the air. It doesn't seem right to have her facedown like that, but he thinks that, considering the circumstances, she would understand.

Once she's in, he stands up and looks around. No one is there. The night looks smudged with darkness. The air is still. A few vacation homes sit across the street half-built, and in the patch of dirt beside them, a group of wood storks raise their heads in unison when the headlights sweep across them. He comes to an abrupt stop at the intersection, then swings slowly onto the main road and heads south. No one is out. The chairs have been stacked up at the café, and the beer signs are all dark at the sports bar. In the homes he passes, there isn't even the blue flickering glow of a television on the bedroom ceiling, and the lot is empty at the church. Only the streetlamps are on, dropping little pools of dim orange light in a line along the shoulder of the road. When Bill reaches the motel, he turns right. It's only a few hundred feet until the asphalt dead-ends at the beach, and he pulls off in the shadow of a pine and cuts the lights.

MOST OF THE Halloween decorations have been taken down at the motel, but some polyester cobwebs remain on the azaleas, a plastic skeleton is still leaning up against one wall in the office, and there's a cleaver with red corn syrup on it by the pool. Only a handful of the rooms are occupied. An anthropologist from Des Moines is dreaming of the 1800s; a husband and wife, both orthodontists, lie in the room next door; and their three children, all in headgear, are in the room after that. There's a breeder of spaniels in one room, and in another, a married man from Sarasota with a graduate student in gender studies from Tampa. All are asleep when Bill opens the gate and walks across the patio to the storage room. No one wakes when the hinges creak, except the youngest child of the orthodontists. Her pillow is cool with saliva, and her headgear is stuck in the fabric of the pillowcase, and she holds her breath while someone shuffles and mutters in the dark outside her window. But she isn't little anymore, she reminds herself, monsters aren't real, and she squeezes her eyes shut.

There are no windows in the storeroom, and Bill can't see a thing. He runs his hands over the objects on one wall—a push broom, a mirror—until his hand finally settles on a shovel. Feeling his way back to the gate, he heads out to where he parked the car along the beach. He keeps to the shadows, with the shovel held neatly by his side, but he doesn't run into anyone. He knows exactly where he is going. He follows the path through the bushes toward the beach, and when it branches, he takes the path to the right. The moon is covered by clouds, and a pavilion comes into view, looking pale and blue in the muted moonlight.

He sits on the bench first, listening. He thinks he hears women gossiping, car doors closing, sirens, rodents stirring in their burrows.

He begins digging discreetly at first, stopping every so often and holding his breath. Soon, though, he is scooping sand out of the hole with hurried, spastic movements. He works his way around the edges, widening and deepening it little by little, as a pile of sand grows beside him. His shirt is soaked through from the effort. It clings to him, and as he digs, he licks the sweat from his upper lip. The muddy sand at the bottom sends up a rich mineral smell. When he's waist-deep, he climbs out and crouches beside it for a moment, looking in, even though there's nothing to see down there.

He drags her out along the path, her body still limp and warm in the sheet, and when they get to the hole, he jumps in first and then pulls her in after him. He wants to position her looking up at the sky, but she won't quite fit that way, so he turns her on her side with her knees tucked up against her chest. He spends some time trying to get his foot out from beneath her until at last, with a violent squirming, he pulls free and scrambles out of the grave. There isn't time to say a prayer. He covers her as quick as he can, kneeling and pushing the pile of sand into the hole with his arms. Then he follows the drag marks on the way to the street, moving his feet back and forth across the sand to erase them.

When he gets home to the apartment, he sits on the couch and stares out into the middle of the room, and the entire night slides rapidly through his mind again: walking down the street in the direction of the apartment, opening the door, the bottle of wine on the counter, the shoes on the floor. He recalls her foot resting against his leg, the rustle of the sheets as they tumbled into bed; flicking the cigarette butt into the bushes; her nose sniffing at his shirt; and her back as she walked away. He arrives at the moment when he makes a fist, then he immediately starts again at the beginning.

He can't find a way to undo it, but neither can he stop himself from trying. He talks to the place where she was lying on the floor and explains that if she had just done this or that differently, things never would have come to this. Then he goes to the fridge for another beer and tries to think of something else.

SABINE'S CAR SITS parked two blocks from their apartment beneath a large pine. On one side of the street is a row of vacant houses; on the other is the Gulf. A raccoon crosses the road to hunt for turtle eggs on the beach, but otherwise no creatures stir. A little before dawn, a pair of headlights appear at the end of the street and swing across the convertible. A deputy is at the end of his shift, making one last sweep of Anna Maria before returning to the office in Bradenton. He parks behind the car and writes out the license plate number on the ticket. Then he pulls himself out of his cruiser and slips the notice under the windshield wiper. He shakes his head. He will never understand if people can't read the NO PARKING sign or if they just don't care.

ALL MORNINGS SOMEHOW are the same. Cats lick their paws. People roll over in bed. Birds fly silently to the sea. The island gets up slowly, and the sun brightens the horizon without heat. A man with a fanny pack and a metal detector heads out past the pavilion to the beach. At the motel, the guests are wrested fitfully from their sleep. The smell of coffee rises and drifts, and down the street, at the café across from the apartment, a truck loads the newspaper machines with the day's edition, and the cinnamon buns go in the oven.

Bill leaves sleep slowly, coming to himself little by little. His back is sore. His hands are raw. Even before he opens his eyes or thinks of last night, a sense of horror descends on him. He knows there is something he doesn't want to think about, and he tries to delay the process of waking. But this only serves to catapult him out of sleep. He finds himself slumped to one side on the couch. The TV is on, and someone is talking about the weather. There's a full beer in his hand, and on the coffee table is the towel he'd been using to clean the blood off the couch. He finishes the beer and closes his eyes, but that only makes it worse.

He can hardly believe the change that's come over the apartment in the few hours he's been asleep. In the closet, her clothes still hang in disorder. Her shampoo is in the shower. The empty wine bottle is on the counter, right where it was before. Everything looks the same, but it no longer feels like somewhere he lives.

THERE'S A BAR on the mainland, a few blocks from a place Bill used to live. He knows the kind of people who drink there, and he backs the car into a spot at the corner of the lot. Before he gets out, he wipes down the steering wheel, the shifter, and the seat belt, and looks around to make sure he hasn't left anything. In the back seat, there's a place where blood has soaked into the cloth, and he pulls a small paring knife out of his backpack and hacks at the spot until he's removed the fabric and the foam beneath it. He puts the chunk of cushion in the first trash can he comes to. As he waits for the bus to take him back to Anna Maria, he thinks about how angry she'd be if she knew he got blood in her car.

WEDNESDAY IS SABINE's day off at the motel. It's a bright, cool, and lovely day, a day like an empty bowl. In such sunshine, all the objects appear to have been placed precisely in their places, even the parrot, dozing on his perch. There isn't much to do so Tom sits out by the pool and pretends to be a guest. Eyes closed, sun warming his face, he imagines this is the last day of his vacation. The wife and kids are still asleep in the room. The van is packed, and by noon they'll be on their way back to Wisconsin or Ontario. There are only a few pages left in his book. If he finishes it before the kids wake up, he can just leave it behind, travel that much lighter. He dozes lightly, following this line of thought, and when the few guests do begin to stir, he almost does call out to them as though he knows them.

The image of Sabine settles on him, but in this watery half-asleep mood, it doesn't trouble him. He considers her as if she's part of an exhibit in a museum. He sees their whole life together this way, far away, at last safely behind glass. Now that the moments have crystallized, with their emotions embedded and intact, it seems to him a lucky, even a beautiful life. They stand beside a sandcastle, its turrets crenellated with shells. The warmth of her hand in his at the courthouse; the hurricane that blew along the coast the day they were married; the rain that beat down on just the two of them, holed up in a hotel room, eating lo mein; even the ways in which she hurt him: all are preserved here, and he doesn't mind them. He is done worrying about her.

The first sign of Bill is a rustling outside the office. Tom finds the man cursing as he tries to extricate himself from the bushes. Bill's eyes move loosely in their sockets, and his shoelaces are untied, but the morning's calm remains with Tom. He waits until Bill has gotten back to his feet unsteadily.

"Have you seen Sabine? We got in a fight last night about my smoking, and she left, and she's not picking up when I call."

"You know how she gets."

"I just—" Bill hitches up his backpack and moves toward him, and the stench of beer and sweat overtakes Tom. "Just tell her I need to talk to her."

Tom stands and watches as the man trips off down the street with his backpack slung over his shoulder. He's done wondering what is going through Bill's head.

THE SCAR ON Robert Corona's temple is from a drunk ex-lineman who robbed him for a handful of quarters. He missed the eye, but he managed to cut some sort of nerve, and now Robert sees only light and dark shapes on the right side. It's like the world's been divided in two, and sometimes he prefers the clear one, and sometimes he prefers the one where dim shapes pull apart and come together without sense or reason. The left eye is the one that works, but when he's trying to tell if someone's lying, it's the other one he turns on them.

Wednesday night, he goes to every dealer he knows, and nobody's selling, so he takes his seventeen dollars down to the Gator Lounge and starts to drink. Two men are talking in low voices

outside the bathroom. The bartender is stubbing out her cigarette in a Styrofoam cup. There's golf on the television and a rock
song on the jukebox. After a few hours, he covers his face with his
hands, and when he takes them away, the bar is empty except for
the bartender and an old man at the corner table with a cigarette
in a long ivory holder.

"One more," Robert says.

"You're broke."

He lifts his arms off the counter and begins counting out the
nickels stuck to his skin, but he gives up just as quickly. The bartender stops stacking glasses.

"Where you staying tonight, Bobby?"

"Oh, don't worry about me." And with a nod at the old man in
the corner, he steps out into the parking lot.

It's a few hours before dawn, and the outside world is as still and
quiet as an empty theater. The lights from the city cast a dull orange glow into the cloudy sky. From the Dumpster by the back fence
comes the smell of curdled milk and wet cigarettes. The blacktop is
still hot under his flip-flops, but there's a cool wind blowing a cup
in circles just outside the door. He gives it a kick and watches as the
wind carries it tumbling away, underneath a white convertible, and
as he stares at the car, he realizes the window is down.

In a second, he's inside it. He runs a finger around the cup
holders, looking for change, and opens the glove box. As he leans
across the seat, he glances up to check if anyone is watching, and
that's when his eye catches the keys glinting in the ignition. He
straightens slowly and reaches out to twist the key. The engine
turns over and grumbles to life, the dials jump and glow on the

dash, and he adjusts the seat until it's comfortable and puts on his belt. He turns on the radio, and by the time he pulls out onto Fourteenth, he's already singing along to the music.

Through the window, a cool breeze seems to carry with it the promise of a different sort of destiny. Robert sees himself cruising down the coast, a cooler in the back full of beer, a girl in the front jiggling amply at every bump, and some slow soul music on the stereo. He sees the car parked outside of motel rooms where women in cowboy outfits tickle him without mercy. There are tables full of barbecued shrimp, hush puppies, ice buckets full of Coke, and there he is in a Panama hat, a girl on each arm, placing fifty-dollar bets at nine to one, slipping twenties into the sweaty palms of valets, smoking his cigarettes out of a long ivory holder, with the car keys in his breast pocket like a talisman. In this mood, he reaches up to adjust the rearview mirror just as the flashers go on behind him.

TWO DEPUTIES STOP by to see Bill around four in the morning on Thursday, but he's so drunk that when they drive away, he can't remember what he just told them. All that day, he hears cruisers pulling into the drive. He is making scrambled eggs when suddenly he is sure the police have surrounded the apartment. He ducks to the ground and crawls to the window. No one is there, and he stands up and brushes off his knees.

When they do come back, just before sunset on Friday, he doesn't expect it at all. He thinks it's the neighbors talking in the courtyard, and when he opens the door, it takes him a few heartbeats to realize it's a sheriff's deputy, dressed in tan and gold, and behind her, three detectives. The deputy is very young, with the slouch of the intelligent and disinterested.

"You here to arrest me?" Bill says.

One of the detectives asks if they can talk to him for a few minutes and have a look around the apartment, and when Bill nods, the deputy puts on blue plastic gloves and brushes past him.

Bill and the detectives sit out in the courtyard. There's a breeze that makes his cigarette burn faster than he'd like.

"Just walk me through Tuesday night," one of the detectives says.

"We had dinner—vegetarian spaghetti. We watched TV. I went out for a cigarette. We got in a fight." There's not much to tell, but Bill feels like he talks for a long time. All three men nod along with what he says, but only the one detective speaks, saying "um-huh" every so often, and taking notes in a small black notebook.

"I tried to get with Tom and say we need to put our heads together."

"Um-huh."

"And find out what's going on, you know?"

"Going on as far as what?"

"Just . . ."

"OK."

"He thinks I hurt her," Bill says. None of the detectives flinch, but Bill senses that some communication passes between them. "Why would I hurt Sabine?"

"Don't know," says the detective.

BRITTA IS IN Germany when the email arrives from Karin. She closes the computer and bites the inside of her cheek.

Missing is a strange word. Hadn't she thought something like this might happen? Hadn't she worried? She realizes she never said goodbye to Sabine before she left. But it is probably nothing. Britta worries too much. That's what Sabine always tells her. She needs to learn to relax, Britta thinks, and she begins cleaning the insides of the cupboards.

THE TROLLEY DRIVER is an enormous man, whalelike in his damp polo shirt, with small considerate eyes, and he is stopped in front of the playhouse when he looks in his mirror and sees a man running down the sidewalk, waving something in his hand. Bill mounts the steps at a run, and nearly falls over as the vehicle lurches forward, only latching on to a railing at the last second.

"I'm looking for someone," he says as they pick up speed. He thrusts the crumpled photo in front of the driver, whose eyes dart back and forth between the photo and the road. "Have you seen her? She's missing."

At the next stop, as a group of sunburned British enter the trolley, the driver takes the picture and looks at it more closely.

"Who is it?"

"My girlfriend," says Bill. "She's missing."

"You know I think I did see someone like this down at Coquina Beach."

Bill stares at the man.

"Yeah, definitely down at Coquina."

"Get me there," he says. "Fast."

The speed limit is twenty-five, and the driver still has to stop every few hundred yards to pick up and drop off passengers, but he goes as fast as he can. Bill takes one of the front seats, and talks to the man about how much he loves his girlfriend, the bike rides they used to take, her cooking, how much he worries about her.

At Coquina, Bill runs up and down the beach with the photograph. He interrupts barbecues and games of paddleball, he talks to a large poodle, and eventually he gives up and walks back north staring mournfully out at the water. *Why isn't Tom out here with his golden retriever looking for Sabine? Where are all her fancy friends with their noses in the air? Where are they now that she needs them most?* It breaks his heart thinking that the only person who truly cares about her is the one who killed her.

THERE'S A WEDDING reception on the beach, and as the sunset draws on, the sounds of polka drift out along the water. High heels lie in pairs here and there on the sand, and a couple strolls off arm and arm into the gloom for a few minutes of privacy before the dancing begins. They speak passionately about nothing in particular, they joke about the bride's cousin, and they are already beside one of the benches before they realize there's a man sitting there asleep with his knees together and his head resting on a small blue backpack. He wakes as they pass by.

"Hang on," he says. His gaze swings between their faces, and his forehead is dripping with sweat. "I'm trying to find a woman. I . . ." He reaches into the backpack and removes a small piece of paper. "Have you seen her?"

He presses the photo into the girl's hands. She wants to help somehow, but she doesn't know what she can say or do.

"I'm sorry," she says. "I wish I could—"

Her boyfriend pulls her away.

BILL WAKES IN the apartment with a stuffy nose, and lies on his back in the bed, looking at the ceiling and breathing. His sternum aches. He has pawned the TV, the radio, his ten-speed, his drill, the blender. What wasn't pawned, the police have seized for evidence: the wine bottle and glass, some cutlery, a blouse.

He's lost her face. He can see her eyes blinking blue and bright in the bathroom mirror when she plucked her eyebrows, and he knows the set of her mouth when she was displeased. He has no trouble recalling her nose or the way she pointed it when angry. But he can't bring these things together. As soon as he draws one into focus, he loses another. Her ears, he has lost entirely, and this, more than anything, depresses him. Her soft little ears, which he would take delicately in his teeth, he had to go find a photo to see what they looked like.

The memory of that night remains with him, but it has changed. In the hours after her death, he could think of nothing but the sequence of events leading up to it. He reviewed each second, every movement of her hand, every note in her voice. No sooner had he finished than he began again. Now he sees that with each of these recollections, the memory of her recedes. The event remains, but it is a clumsy caricature, in which he and Sabine walk around like marionettes. The steadily mounting anger and the terror that came with it, he no longer feels these when he remembers her tying her shoelaces.

AT BRITTA'S APARTMENT on Anna Maria Island, no one answers the bell, but a neighbor rolls down her car window just far enough to tell Bill that Britta's in Germany for the week. He walks past the motel and sees Tess talking on the phone, but he's not

allowed on the property. When Karin finds him, he's back in the
courtyard at the apartment with a case of beer between his feet.
She leaves her car door open and the engine running.

"I've already been yelled at," he says. "But if you want, I can tell
you the same thing as everybody else."

"You're still staying here?"

"Long as I can."

"Until the end of the month?"

He nods and, for the first time, looks her in the face. "You
think it was me?"

"Could be," she says, and digs a cigarette out of her purse.

"What do you think happened?"

"I don't know. I try not to think about it."

"You don't think about her?" he says.

"You do?"

"Every minute."

"Well," she says. "That's good to do."

WHO HASN'T RESENTED a woman? Who hasn't wanted to
cut off his pinkie and make her see it, saying, "You did this." Who
hasn't looked up at the full moon and wished it would fall on her?

Bill eyes the bartender as though she can read his thoughts,
and he worries over a mound of boiled peanuts. Around three, the
room begins to fill. A few kids at first, then the regulars, shriveled
up like old palmetto leaves, take their positions. The tourists come
last, smelling of steak and SPF. They leave the door open too long,
and a breeze sends paper napkins swirling around the bartender.

Bill hides in the back room by the pool table, where it's quiet,
near the chalk and quarters and graffiti. There's a chunk of hard-

boiled egg on the table, and a single ant has been left to itself to figure out what to do with it.

Two boys come in, blond-haired and smooth-cheeked. In their long surf shorts, they seem to be leaning backward.

"Is this your table?"

Bill looks up.

"Hey," says the other. "Are you still on here?" His hand shoved deep in his shorts, he's jingling a whole pocketful of quarters.

"Yes, I am," says Bill.

The chalk shoots up in a plume as he strikes the cue ball. The solids and stripes sort themselves out. He finishes off the kid in a few quick strokes. Pulling long slugs of beer between shots, he dismisses the friend, as well. Feeling flush, he goes to get another drink, and when he comes back, he finds some tourists fingering the cues.

"I'm on here right now," he says.

Again the crack of balls, the feeding of dollars into the machine by the bathroom, and the *clink-clink* of dispensed coins. He leans on the cue like a crutch.

"I used to be all right," he says to someone leaning against the wall. "Hung around with my old man at the pool hall. Now look at this. They call this English." He tilts the cue down steeply toward the table. "Are you looking?"

He loses a few games then but comes back with another beer and a cup of quarters. Soon he's playing with a young woman. "Now the trick," he says, "is to get down low like this. You've got to sight her along the cue. Otherwise, you're just guessing."

She doesn't say anything.

"That's it," he says. "That's the big secret." He looks around, but there's no one left in the room except the woman's boyfriend.

"It's your shot," the man says.

"Yes," Bill says, settling down behind the cue ball and drawing the table into focus. "Now, who's solids and who's stripes?"

THE ROUGH NAP of green baize, and how it feels to regain life there, the smells of the bar—the yeast, the urine, the smoke and congealed fat, the perfume—all concentrated by the billiard cloth. His cheek is chalky and numb. His eye rolls back as if to see his ear. He finds the bathroom, pisses, vomits, hums a tune, leans his head against the mirror. It's still light outside. A few hours have passed, but not much else. The sun has just begun its march on the horizon, and at last the sky is darkening. The pavilion is ahead. He talks to her and thinks, if only she'd known how he feels now, so bored and so lonely.

16: Laurel and Bay

IN THE DAYS AFTER Sabine Musil-Buehler disappeared, the detectives took a number of photographs out on Anna Maria, and during the time that I was following the case, I kept a folder of these images in a drawer in my desk and returned to them every so often when I felt I'd lost a sense of what I was doing. There was nothing gruesome about the pictures, and if someone had stumbled upon the folder, they would hardly have thought these bland images depicted the denouement of a fatal love affair. There was a shot of the island from above, a shot of the motel, a shot of the door to Sabine and Bill's apartment. There was a photograph of Tom and one of Bill. Tom stands in his living room. He wears a black shirt, his hands are at his waist, and as he stares into the lens of the camera, he bites his lip. Bill stands in the apartment in front

of the couch, his eyes downcast and his face expressionless. He
has a pen in the pocket of his shirt, a pair of sunglasses hanging
from his top button, and two large circles of sweat spreading out
under his arms. The photos were taken with a flash, and because
of this, both men's shadows are outlined on the walls behind them.
In one image, the convertible sits in a patch of sand and crabgrass
at the impound lot, looking clean and white. In the background,
there are other cars, each presumably with a crime and a story of
its own.

I was drawn to these images, I think, precisely because of how
commonplace they seemed. There was a photo of the floor of
Sabine's car, where an *Ultimate Santana* album had come to rest,
and one of a closet, with a few outfits hanging—a yellow cotton
skirt, a black-and-white dress—and below them, a jumble of high
heels and open shoe boxes and a fallen coat hanger. In the open
trunk of the convertible, there are Styrofoam plates, a snorkel, a few
plastic bags, and a single shoe. On a side table, there is scorecard for
a board game, an empty wine bottle, and a remote control. They
reminded me of the aimless photographs that children take, confusing precisely because it is impossible to say just why they were
taken. They seemed almost like they could have come from any life.
There wasn't anything extraordinary about the photographs of the
couch in the apartment, a long red sofa with its cushions disheveled, except that in one of the photos a few small plastic placards
with the numbers 2 and 3 indicated where blood had fallen.

IN THE MONTHS following that summer visit to Florida,
while Erin and I went about our lives in Iowa, I began assembling
the notes I'd made on my flight. I kept up with the goings-on in

Anna Maria. I spoke sometimes with the detectives and emailed with Sabine's friends and family. I continued writing small postcards to Bill Cumber and received long letters in return. Gradually, these letters trailed off of their own accord. Robert Corona was sentenced for grand theft auto, served his time, and shortly after his release, was arrested while driving a stolen van down Fourteenth Street. The lead detective retired and took a part-time job at a local school. On the anniversary of her disappearance, Tom and a few friends organized a quiet memorial service for Sabine, which for lack of a grave, they held in a shadeless garden beside city hall.

The state attorney's office quietly brought charges against Bill Cumber for the murder, but the evidence was so insubstantial—no body, no weapon, no motive—that neither the prosecution nor the defense seemed to be in any rush to actually carry out a trial. At one docket sounding after another, the court date was postponed. By that time, I had given up hoping that a trial would bring any sort of closure to the case. What would it have meant anyway if Bill Cumber were found guilty or not guilty? Sabine would still be missing. I had ceased to expect there would be news, and in many ways, I felt a great deal of relief when I thought that I could finally put the story behind me, that I would never again be obliged to visit Florida.

Hardly had this thought crossed my mind when I received a call from the assistant state attorney. Some of the details in Bill's letters to me conflicted with the account he'd given detectives. Nothing substantial really, the attorney assured me, but a small part of the puzzle. I would soon be receiving a subpoena to testify.

So I made one final journey to Florida. I wanted to review the

case the state had prepared in advance of the trial, and I waited
for some time outside the state attorney's office before a side door
finally opened and one of the administrative assistants waved me
into the rooms beyond. She pushed before her a cart stacked high
with boxes as she led me through the offices.

"You wanted to look at the materials from the Cumber case,
right? We'll just put you in the conference room."

"What do you have there?" I said. "Looks heavy."

She smiled at me. "This is the Cumber case."

For three days, I went through the boxes one by one. Even now,
it's difficult for me to say exactly what I was looking for. There
were affidavits from Sabine's friends, deputies' reports, the transcription of Tom Buehler's polygraph examination, a copy of the
first letter I'd sent to Bill, reams and reams of paper, but there was
hardly anything I didn't already know, and the more I read, the
more I felt I was doing nothing more than making myself ill. It
seems to me now that there wasn't any real reason to look through
those files. There were obvious signs that their love affair would
end terribly, signs that many had understood from the start.

Tom Buehler had predicted as much, and in his deposition,
he'd recalled a conversation he had with Sabine when she first
started dating Bill.

> We're in my backyard. I said, Sabine, he's a con man. I said here's
> what's going to happen. When he gets out of prison, I said, I'll
> give you two months, and he's going back into doing this old
> stuff again. He's going to cause trouble at the motel. He's going to
> cause trouble for you and trouble for me. I said my whole concern
> is when you two break up, and it's going to happen, he is going to

be big trouble. And she's trying to explain to me why she's doing all this. And she says I can't help it, I fell in love.

I think it was this: she'd loved him, and she thought that was enough. I wanted there to be some evidence that she hadn't been wrong all along. Sabine believed in what Carol Wood had called "the recuperative nature of love," and I wanted to believe, too.

That night, after a dinner alone at a bar in Bradenton, I called Erin from my hotel room.

"If people lived a thousand years," I said, "how many do you think would stay together?"

"Not many," she said. "But probably a few."

THERE IS ANOTHER possible reason that I sifted through those files with such thoroughness: I knew that when I finished, I would have to drive to the county jail a few miles north of the city and speak with Bill Cumber, who was there awaiting the trial. I didn't want to see him, not because I was disgusted by what it seemed he'd done, but because I didn't think I could bring myself to ask him about it again. I put off the trip one day, then another. That Wednesday, as I was finally preparing to make the drive, I received a message on my phone, letting me know there would be no trial, the case was now closed. William Cumber had just confessed.

The confession took place in downtown Bradenton, on one of the upper floors of the Manatee County Judicial Center. He was brought in a little before ten in the morning, and he sat down with his appointed attorney, the representatives of the state, a number of detectives, and a stenographer. In response to the state attorney's questions, Bill began to tell a story that was, by and large, exactly as the detectives had imagined it. He and Sabine had quarreled the night she disappeared. He had been drinking beer. She had been drinking wine. He went out for a cigarette, and when he returned to the apartment, she confronted him about his smoking. In the argument that ensued, she said she was leaving him, and she began to dress. She put on her jeans and her shirt. She was sitting on the couch, tying her sneakers, when he struck her twice, once with his left hand, on the head, then a second time with his right hand. He was unable to say where the second blow fell. He knew only that it landed somewhere on her face. Before she had time to react, he placed his hands around her throat.

How long would you say you were choking her? the attorney interrupted. *A minute? More?*

Bill searched for words. *Until she wasn't moving.*

He looked down at her afterward. He couldn't believe what he'd done, but he knew that he couldn't go back to prison, so he came up with a plan. He took a sheet off the bed and wrapped her in it. After he'd looked outside to make sure that no one was around, he took her out to where her car was parked.

Did you drag her or throw her over your shoulder?

I drug her.

And put her in the back seat?

Yes.

It's been said she was very particular about whom she let drive her car. Is that true?

That's true.

He drove a half mile south and turned onto Eighty-First Street, and in a shadowed part of the road just past her motel, he parked.

After stealing a shovel from the motel, he went out to the beach and began to work. In that sand, the softest in the world according to the visitors' bureau, it took only twenty minutes to dig a hole up to his waist, and when he'd finished burying her, he drove back up the island, parked down the street from the apartment, and went home. The next afternoon, he drove the car across the Cortez Bridge into Bradenton and left it at the Gator Lounge, where Robert Corona would later find it. Just before dark, he caught the last bus back to the island. He was lying in bed when the convertible was pulled over.

As part of the plea agreement, Bill was required to show the exact location of the body, and when the confession concluded, he was driven out to the island in an unmarked Crown Victoria. He led the way to the beach, followed by a group of deputies, a SWAT team, a number of reporters, and the spokesman for the sheriff's office. Taking small steps, because of the shackles, he led them to a pavilion where he and Sabine had often watched the sunset together, and he pointed to the ground. They dug four inches at a time, running everything through a metal sieve, and late that afternoon, they uncovered a Converse sneaker. A forensic anthropologist arrived the next morning, and during the course of the day Friday, with brushes and fine picks, and with the help of two graduate students, a skeleton was carefully removed from the sand. It was transported to the office of the medical examiner in Sarasota, and based on comparisons with her dental records, it was quickly identified as Sabine Musil-Buehler.

I watched the video of Bill leading the deputies to the body again and again, and I listened to the confession enough times that I could recite whole sections of it from memory. I knew that the anthropologist, inexplicably, wore the same gardening gloves as my great-aunt. I knew that Bill wore socks beneath his sandals and that as he was being returned to the cruiser, one of the detectives picked a burr from his clothing. I knew the syncopated clacking of the stenographer in the background, and I knew when Bill would reach across the microphone, drowning out all the voices with the jangling of his cuffs. I knew the sigh of the assistant state attorney, who seemed to understand exactly how the questioning should proceed but not why. But more than anything, there was one moment a few minutes into the confession that always made me stop the tape. It was the moment just before the murder. Sabine had begun to put her clothes on. Bill followed her out of the bedroom. She sat on the couch tying her shoes. The entire conversation had taken place in the past tense, and the attorney wanted to know what happened then, how did the murder begin, and suddenly Bill slips into present tense. "I lose control," he says, and the past ceases to be past.

ON THE BEACH, I met again with the reporter from the island paper. She had her ball cap pulled down, and even though the case was at a conclusion, she spoke in rapid sentences, as if she felt she was still on deadline.

"Bizarre," she said, looking out at the water. "That's how I would describe it. He buried her under the pavilion where they'd always watch the sunset. I'm sure you heard the confession, the way he described why he chose the spot. 'The least unexpected place,' he said. If you go down there and look around, that pavilion sticks out like a sore thumb. It's the only thing that catches your eye. If I've killed someone, do I put the body where someone can find it, or where no one ever will? It's crazy to bury her there."

"Then why do you think he did?"

"I keep asking myself that question. It's the absolute worst place to dispose of a body. I don't know. Sometimes I think he wasn't trying to get rid of her. Sometimes I think he wanted to know exactly where she was."

We stood to leave. She took off her hat and ran a hand through her hair.

"You heard what happened with Detective Gisborne, I'm guessing? He's retired, you know. He and his wife were supposed to fly to Europe. They'd been planning the vacation I don't know how long. The morning their flight was supposed to leave, Cumber confesses and leads the deputies out to the beach."

"Did they go to Europe?"

"What do you think?"

It was a Saturday when I finally made my way to the county jail, and the road was busy with an estate auction. In the clusters of cars, I drove back and forth along that stretch of highway three or four times before I saw a small sign indicating the way to the jail. The road ran straight for a time, then turned abruptly and crossed a set of railroad tracks, where a tattooed man in a flat-brimmed ball cap was walking without haste in the general direction of Tampa. Then it followed an embankment of gypsum, covered in fine yellow grass and wildflowers. Through the moss-draped oaks, a few low buildings like barracks appeared briefly, flashing white in the sunshine, then vanished behind the greenery.

At last, a wooden sign directed me to a parking lot, and a long barrel building with chain link over its windows and a door at either end.

The line was short. Very soon, I was given a number and waved through the metal detector into the room beyond. Two aluminum benches ran the length of the space. At intervals on the walls, a series of metal boxes was mounted, each numbered and containing a screen about the size of a sheet of paper, and a heavy plastic receiver of the kind one used to find in public telephone booths. As I waited, the room began to fill: women mostly, mostly young, some alone, some with children. At exactly nine o'clock, the screens blinked gray, and each person sat up and took the receiver off the hook. I took up my own receiver, and the screen in front of me flickered and showed Bill Cumber.

"You know," he said, and I knew that he was speaking of Sabine. "In the long run, I don't think it would've ever worked out."

THE WHITE FARMHOUSE still sits on Dodge Street in Iowa City. The neighbor still collects towels at the end of each semester, and launders and folds them and stows them in the cab of his truck. He is planning to have a big sale, he says, but he doesn't know how much to charge. The Realtor is still trying to buy the neighbor's property. She wants to tear down both houses and put up an apartment building. Everything is still in its place, except that Erin and I no longer live in that house. I couldn't bring myself to go up the stairs the last time I visited—from the street, I could see a big screen playing football in the living room, and a jersey draped over the railing of the porch—but as I stood there, I remembered one afternoon when a woman had appeared at our front door.

Erin was at work, and I was at my desk, and for a long time I didn't hear the gentle knocking in the other room. The door was open, but the woman, tall and stooped, hadn't wanted to intrude.

"I used to live here," she said. "Do you mind if I look around?"

Out on the street, a man in glasses sat in an idling car while she walked from one room to the next, saying nothing, touching nothing, only angling her head this way and that.

"It's just like it was," she said. "I lived here till I was six, then we moved up to Prairie du Chien." She put a hand on the wall of the living room. "Even the walls are the same color."

She made it back to the doorway. The man in the car was watching us closely, but she seemed unable to cross back over the threshold, as though there were something she wanted to express but she didn't know what it was.

I said, "Do you have fond memories?"

"Oh." She wrapped her arms around herself. "Some good, some bad."

THE ELECTRONIC BELLS begin to toll at the church on Pine Avenue. It is almost dark on the beach. The joggers' shadows keep pace alongside them, and the wind blows in for no good reason except to bring the smell of salt and fish. The terns have lined up along the water, looking west, and a few boats crash impatiently across the swells, and all at once, the couples stop to wait for sunset. Here and there, a cloud is touched with orange, and along the horizon to the north and south, the pale-blue cumulus stretches out in a line, like cutouts of an endless pilgrimage.

Bill sits in the pavilion rubbing his eyes with the backs of his wrists. His skin is pale, and his lips are white and cracked. He has a backpack on the bench beside him, and he cradles an open can of beer between his legs. He has his eyes on the sunset, but he hardly sees it. She is there, directly beneath his feet. His mouth moves. He is speaking very softly. Of what? To whom? If someone were to stop him, he couldn't say.

He knows he should go home, eat some dinner, take a nap. He knows a million things he ought to do, but he can't think of any reason to do them. Now would be the time to escape. And now, and now. Instead, he smokes one cigarette after another and spins the strike wheel on his lighter.

THERE IS A woman. Slightly broad-shouldered, she stands with her feet set apart, like a dancer or a gymnast, or like someone slightly angry. I've seen her at rush hour on the platform opposite my own, her hair hanging down across her cheek as she reads a book, turning the pages with a quick rasping sound, not looking up as the train squeals into the station and disgorges its passengers, not looking up until the last minute, when, with a little leap—and jeté—she slips between the closing doors. At midnight, driving down the back roads of Pennsylvania, with the rain coursing out of the sky, I've seen her between flicks of the wiper blades, in the dented sedan going the other direction. She's the woman one glimpses, the woman one sees reflected in mirrors, the flash of hair in sunlight, the outrageous laugh that rings in a crowded restaurant and never stops ringing.

In my dreams, where the architecture is arranged not in accordance with physical laws but by the edict of feelings, I leave a college class and step into the grove of sequoias I so often imagined as a child, or the pool where I once learned to dive is now in the middle of an expressway full of parked cars. Sabine no longer appears to me, but if the dream lasts long enough, this other woman finds me there. She sits next to me in the back of a van eating unripe mangoes, or she does the dead man's float while I swim laps. She leads me through a home that seems to dissolve at its edges into jungle; or in a motel in the mountains, she sits by a window writing a letter while I lie in bed watching her hand move slowly across the page. The sinews of that hand run straight to my heart, and I know with a sort of wistful regret that I must throw over whatever life I have been living and stay here in this room and simply be in love with her forever. I rise then and walk to her, and draw the hair back from her face. She begins to turn her head, and as if my vision is unable to bear the weight of my own desires, the colors shift, the shapes crumble, and I am awake again in bed.

The density of life insists upon coincidence. That my grandfather should die, that I should go home to make my peace with him and instead find Erin, that two lovers in Florida should fall one night into a pointless argument, and that sometime later the man should bury the woman's body near a motel where I once stayed, these are matters almost purely of chance. And yet by virtue of having occurred in my life around the same time, these disparate events become part of the same story. A fire takes the shape of the person describing it, and the very breath and texture of life lies in the simple work of trying to understand how one day relates to the next. It has not gone unrealized by me that as I fumbled so earnestly with the story of Bill and Sabine, I was also undertaking a not unrelated investigation into my own life. In point of fact, perhaps, nothing has been more at the forefront of my mind as I assembled this account than the day-to-day experience of my own snuffling attempts to be pleasant, attempts that, over the course of time, cohered into a real and actual woman, a set of pots and pans, a houndstooth couch, and a small but bright apartment on a tree-less street in New York City.

I know that the figure who attends my dreams does not exist, never has nor will, and yet there are moments with Erin—she is a thousand miles away, or maybe she has only stepped behind the shower curtain, or we are on the couch, beneath an old orange blanket, her head against my chest, her eyes closed, my own eyes closing, too—moments when I am afraid to draw back the curtain, afraid to wake her, when I must hold her head tightly to me because I feel that no sooner than I see her, she will disappear. In a very real way, this book, which I have written merely in the hopes of understanding what it means to love another human being, has been composed for her, in the moments when she was sleeping.

The world is replete with beautiful things. Lilacs perfume the garden, tractors plow the field, the pillows have been fluffed, a soft rain falls along the coast; there are newborn calves, ferny creeks, songs of melancholy and of innocence; the eggs are fresh, the cream is cool, a woodpecker hammers in the hickories; the canoe noses in the reeds, looking for a place to moor, and a rocket ship plunges through the vacuum of space; the factories prom-ise silk and steel, the horizon promises the night; there are av-enues of corn where a child can walk till dark and not see another human soul, and avenues of wristwatches and purses down which we stroll to the art museum to see the exhibition on Le Corbusier; in winter, there are fires, in summer, winds, and in spring and fall, the geese fly home beside the moon and wake a thousand miles of lovers. We must fly to those we love. Anoint them with oil, adorn them patiently with laurel and bay. That I could have been better. That this yearning might snub oblivion. That I would be judged by the tenderness I now feel and by nothing else. This is the hope. This is the wish imparted by my hand, as it grazes your shoulder, in the moment before we wake.